Endorsements

This book represents Jasmine's passion and her perspective on prayer. It is a labor of love that she sends forth with praise and thanksgiving to her Lord and Savior. Read this book and see what it does to spiritually invigorate your life. Experience Jasmine's insights on the dynamics of prayer and be blessed as you journey through the pages of this inspirational volume.

Pastor Garfield Danclar,
Educate to Liberate Ministry (ELM)

Jasmine writes about praying from the heart; she inspires and teaches us how to listen to God. She is an inspiration to me and others around her. I believe my own prayers were answered when I met Jasmine who has become a friend and has shown me how to stay strong even in adverse situations. She is restoring my hope again in prayers and the faith to remain positive in my life. She truly has a gift to share and I hope others feel the same and read her words. With God all things are possible.

Michele Paccione, Council Member
of the City of Palm Bay

Appropriately dubbed the "fire woman," Prophetess Jasmine Gordon is a woman that knows God, listens to Him, and spares no effort to spend time in His presence. Her book *Fear Not, There is Still Power in Prayer* is a testament that prayer is the Christian's food for the soul; the way of deliverance, comfort in times of trouble and victory over Satan and all his demons. Best of all, prayer is God's way to commune with Him.

Evangelist W. P.

T0208544

TO: _____

From: _____

Thanks for your support. May God continue to bless you and your family unlimitedly with good health, wealth and uncommon favor.

Fear Not! There Is Still Power in Prayer

Jasmine Gordon

WestBow
PRESS
A DIVISION OF THOMAS NELSON

Edited by Shawna E. Brown.

For contacts: www.fearnott.com
e-mail. Fearnot46@yahoo.com
Tel. (718) 781- 0671
804)720-6080
(813) 210-3686

WestBow Press books may be ordered through booksellers or by contacting:

WestBow Press
A Division of Thomas Nelson
1663 Liberty Drive
Bloomington, IN 47403
www.westbowpress.com
1 (866) 928-1240

ISBN: 978-1-4908-1193-2 (sc)

Library of Congress Control Number: 2013919194

Printed in the United States of America.

WestBow Press rev. date: 10/23/2013

Dedication Page

This book is proudly dedicated to my son Navarone Reid (Javin) who has been a tremendous inspiration in the completion of this project. Javin has not yet surrendered his life to the will of Christ but my dreams for his life is that he will accept his prophetic calling to evangelism. Baby boy you are the apple of my eye.

To my dear mother who relentlessly nurtured my consciousness in salvation and whose unending prayers kept me alive today. Her inspiration allowed me to appreciate and understand the power of prayer. Because of her firm foundation in my upbringing, I am who I am today. I love you momma.

Epigraph Page

"Nobody can say how he shall die, but everybody must decide how and for what he shall live" *Jose Rizal*

"A positively engaged mind is a productive, happy, renewed and peaceful mind. Keep your mind occupied." *Jasmine Gordon*

Table of Contents

Foreword

By Shawna Brown

*I*t is not every day that one is given the opportunity to write a foreword; especially a foreword on the power of prayer. So when it was requested of me, I asked myself, Lord what would you want me to relay on a book about the effectiveness of prayer. The answer came back very clearly. Why not answer the question on just how effective prayer has been in your own life.

There is no art in praying. God answers the smallest prayers and He understands the simplest prayers. What He really pays attention to is the sincerity of the prayer and the faith through which that prayer is uttered. Sometimes, however, we wonder if God really hears our prayer and if He does why does it seem that He does not answer or take so long to answer. While God understands and hears every single prayer that is uttered unto Him, there are other factors that may affect where, when and how our prayers are answered. In the Old Testament book of Daniel, the scriptures said that God heard and answered Daniels prayer but the messenger God sent to deliver the answer to Daniel was delayed by the prince of Persia. Who is delaying your prayer? What is standing in the way of your deliverance and your happiness? In her first unprecedented novel *"Fear Not, There is Still Power in Prayer,"* Evangelist Nichole "Jasmine" Gordon answer some of these fundamental questions and shed some light on these age old mysteries.

I write this foreword with ease because I know firsthand the effectiveness of fervent prayer. When I nearly lost my life two years ago by an attack from the enemy, it was the prayer of my mother that reached God's ear when He pulled me out of my situation and gave me another chance to live. This near-death experience in my life was not a fairy tale or some story that was relayed to me, it was what I lived and experienced firsthand. Prayer works! It is with this firm belief that I write to you and encourage you to never stop praying. Yes, there are times when the enemy tries to discourage praying by making you feel that your efforts are futile and of no consequence. But, I urge you to persevere. I urge you to continue to pray, without ceasing, because it is in prayer that believers can yield results.

Jasmine Gordon relays just how powerful a tool prayer is in the believers' warfare. Her book gives a direct glimpse into what prayer is and what we can do to enhance our prayer lives. She reminds us of the unconscious behaviors that may be hindering our prayers and teaches us how to take control of any situation, obstacle or dilemma in our personal lives. This book is every believers guide to getting their prayers answered. It is a relevant must-read for beginners learning how to pray and a re-assurance for veteran prayer warriors everywhere. If not for yourself, then pray for the benefit of a loved one or a friend; you may be the voice that God listens to on behalf of those that cross your path. I join in agreement with the songwriter and declare that "somebody prayed for me; they had me on their mind; they took the time and prayed for me."

I urge you to take the time and pray for someone and when you have finished praying for them, pray for yourself. This book encourages you to pray for your children and friends of your children; it teaches you how to pray for your relationships; Pray for your co-workers; Pray for your enemies or those that spitefully try to harm you; Pray for your world leaders and for your church leaders; Pray, pray and pray again. Your break-thru is just a prayer away. What have you got to fear when you have the power of prayer?

Preface
Author's Reflection:
From My Heart to Yours

J began this journey with no particular goal in mind. For one, I am not a novel writer seeking the benefit of fame or fortune from fictitious stories embellished with plots, characters and a fated protagonist who heroically saves the day at the end of the storyline.

No, my experiences are closely attuned with reality. I am simply one individual, a vessel, that allowed God to manifest His work through me so that perhaps other individuals and vessels may find inspiration.

This project specifically speaks to those who are in need of encouragement and those lacking inspiration to incite the effectual fervor of prayer: To those who have come to a spiritual desert in their walk with Christ or those broken in spirit from the plights of spiritual warfare. Yes, this message seeks to testify to the spiritually malnourished suffering from spiritual thirst, spiritual hunger, spiritual deafness and blindness and those held captive against their will in a perpetual cycle of hopelessness.

There are those who have grown weary and tired of organized religion and traditional rituals that seldom avail any enlightenment but instead stagnate and perplex individuals. There is a message here for such a person.

I can testify to the power in prayer because it is the reason I am alive today. Had it not been for the undefeated power of effective, fervent prayer, I would not have had the strength to withstand the many attacks that encompassed my life. Death had a pre-established place saved for me but it was not because it was my fate to die early but because of the many fiery darts and assaults that the enemy launched towards me in retaliation. Through prayer, I am able to pen my testimony to these pages and herald for the world to hear that I can celebrate and shout victory because prayer made me, kept me and is still keeping me alive.

A few years ago, I managed to hear a man in conversation on the radio calling himself Jesus. He asserted that repentance is not necessary because there is no Satan or sin. Neither is there any heaven or eternal damnation so the use for prayer should be obsolete. His way of thinking is what seems to have taken over the church causing an epidemic into what I refer to as the backsliding syndrome. Satan is working tirelessly and with much success through characters heard on the radio and seen on television to foster lies to overhearing listeners.

First, prayers were abolished in the schools. Secondly, more and more church goers are finding it difficult to commit to a steady prayer life. Just take a glimpse into the average believers' schedule. The majority of the day is usually pre-occupied with work or some form of means to earn a living. Then, the demand of home is next on our agenda of things to do: preparation of dinner, helping the children with schoolwork or having to complete a homework assignment of our own. Throughout this time, we are encumbered with numerous cellular phone activities from texting to conversations and the list continues. Let's face it, our lives are filled with distractions. And even if after tending to our personal needs we would carve out some time for prayer, we are still faced with other time consuming distractions such as Facebook, Twitter and checking emails. God forbid we get behind with keeping up with the social networks. My intention is not to be sarcastic but my point is that the distractions are limitless and everyone is busy. But, it is up to us as individuals to place prayer as a priority on our hectic to-do list.

I have found that the distractions will not go away. In fact, believers must find it necessary to customize a time of prayer and fellowship with the Lord in order to strengthen their spiritual growth. Simply put, it is called prioritizing. Certainly, it seems more entertaining to check what new program is on the television or to see who has posted new messages to Facebook but neither of these social choices can uplift the soul.

I encourage you not to fall for the deception brought on by the powers of darkness. Prayer is the only weapon believers have against attacks. However, entertaining as it may seem, Facebook cannot save souls. It cannot turn pimps into preachers or prostitutes into evangelists. Enticing as our email may be; Yahoo, Gmail, or Hotmail cannot turn gunmen into soul winners nor can it persuade drug dealers to become missionaries. Thank God for the few people who utilize this social media as a channel to encourage and enlightened others. Prayer is the only weapon in the Christian arsenal that stops Satan and his comrades in their tracks. Prayer uproots every wicked seed planted by the enemy. It cancels every demonic contract and strips them of their death assignment. Prayer confuses the enemy and frustrates their counsel because evil cannot overcome the power of prayer.

Have you been praying about a certain situation in your life? Have you contritely confessed your sins and is now arduously praying for healing, deliverance or financial freedom? Have you continued searching the scriptures for every biblical reference pertaining to your situation to no avail? I encourage you to press along and to keep persevering, consistently dedicated to the word of God. In the book of Mark 11:24, the word reminds us of this: [24]Therefore I say unto you, [what things soever ye desire], when ye pray, believe that ye receive them, and ye shall have them. (KJV)

Believing without first seeing only strengthens your faith in Christ. Remember that nothing happens overnight but before the day is over and before the night has ended, God is working things out in your favor. When your faith leaves you discouraged, remember the man with the infirmity sitting by the pool for thirty-eight years (St. John 5:5) or the woman who suffered for twelve years with the issue of blood (Mark 5:5) or countless others who have suffered atrocities, sickness or even death but never stopped believing that God is able. Their suffering was rather long but they never quit. Instead, they positioned themselves to cease an opportunity of deliverance from the only one capable of making them whole again, Jesus Christ.

Perhaps you were expecting to reach further in life through faith you have placed in someone or something. Or have invested your time and money into things that yielded no results. Can you recall the story about Joseph and the butler in Genesis 40: 20-23? Having been released from prison, the butler had forgotten about Joseph for two years. At the end of the two years, a problem manifested that nobody else but Joseph could solve. Not only was the butler forced to remember Joseph, he was compelled to recommend him to the King. I want to say to you that whatever it is you have faced in your life or are currently facing, it is just a process to position you for your future. If you are not where you thought you should be it may be because your season has not yet come. You are valuable in the kingdom of God and He will not allow you to become useless or trampled by your own fears. Wait for your name to be called and for the Lord to open the doorway for you. After all, nobody else can do what you were appointed and anointed to do. Again I say, wait for your time and do not cease to pray.

For those of you suffering from addictions or can't seem to break a crippling habit, you would be surprised to know that prayer can replace your most stifling addiction. Victory does not usually come without a fight or by waving a magic wand. But once you are equipped with the right tools, you are certain to come out victorious.

This book is to incite you to the wisdom in praying. It is by divine revelation that I gather these thoughts and relay them to you. It is meant to encourage you to get back into your prayer closet and spend more quality time with God. The same God who performed numerous miracles through Moses, Elijah, Ezekiel or Daniel is the same God who can use you to perform miracles right now.

It is only a matter of time before your worldly possessions are of no use to you. Wealth nor fame, intellect nor accolades cannot do anything for the sanctity of your soul but prayer it will be your most valuable asset. Get involved with prayer now as your redemption quickly nears to a close. The Lord is on His way back to redeem His people. Will he find you praying?

Pray!

Acknowledgments

I would like to extend my appreciation and deepest respect to my pastor and first lady David and Marilyn Taylor and to the Harvest Time Seventh Day Church of God family for their love, prayers and encouragement. Much blessings and favor upon you all.

Special thanks to my sister and best friend Joy Gordon-Dodd, whose spiritual, physical and financial support has been a guiding force in my life. Sis, without you I would not have embarked on this journey and your efforts did not go unnoticed or unappreciated.

Also to my other siblings Eula, Ruby, Celes, Evelyn, Ricky, and Norman thanks for the love, prayers and the best wishes. In sweet, precious, un-forgettable memories of my brother Errol Gordon (Henry) who has allowed me to understand a little more about God and His love.

Thanks to all my family: nieces, nephews, aunts and cousins, thanks for the respect, love and admiration.

Pauline Fisher-Walker thanks for always being there for me. I love you.

I am eternally grateful for those who have placed their pride aside to expose their personal struggles and weaknesses for the testimonial data in this book. I applaud you for your courage to allow others insight into your challenges so that they too can overcome.

To my biggest cheerleaders: Jean Bradford (Angel) in Florida, Jenifer Gooden in Jamaica and pastor Marlene McGriff in Vero Beach Florida, unlimited blessings to you.

To my exceptionally talented editor Shawna Brown who went beyond the call of duty to ensure my dream becomes a reality. Thank you for your bravery in taking on my projects. Relentlessly, you delved with patience to bring out the best in my writings. You are an asset and a writers dream. Our meeting was divinely orchestrated.

Margaret O'Shaughnessy, words are not enough to say how grateful I am to have you in my life and as a prayer partner. Thank you for giving up so much of yourself. You have given a new meaning to the word giving. May abundant blessings be upon you and your family! Love you.

To my spiritual mothers, teachers, mentors and counselors for their prayers and encouragement: Thank you for everything you have instilled in me.

Thanks to Jeff and David from WestBow Press. I embrace your professionalism and words of encouragement towards this project. Thank you for not giving up on me.

To Mr. Lee Von Nutall, I am very grateful to have you on my team and in my corner.

And finally, a warm thank you to my prospective readers who, by lending their financial support in the purchase of this book, will sow into this ministry. May God bless and keep you all.

Introduction

ear Not! There is Still Power in Prayer. Fear is a destructive weapon that the enemy uses to cripple the body of Christ into silence. Fear causes us to compromise the word and the work of God. *"Fear Not! There is Still Power in Prayer"* offers the believer a guide to withstand the wiles and attacks of the enemy through effective fervent prayer. But, before we can get to the point where our prayers become effective, we must look inward and perform a self cleaning test to uproot some of the ailments that causes our prayer lives to be lacking.

Do not be afraid! Worry, panic, intimidation and doubt usually stems from our own insecurities or fears which can wreck havoc on our spiritual weaponry. As a believer, you are equipped with the power to bind principalities and powers, demote authority, defuse bombs and take dominion in destroying the plan of the enemy.

Although each believers walk with Christ is specific to that individual, we can learn from examples of those that walked before us. Peter defied the odds of gravity by walking on water simply because of his focus on Jesus Christ. However, even Peter realized that he was doing what was humanly impossible and the moment he allowed fear to distract him, he began to sink. Later we learn that even though he was one of Jesus' beloved disciples, Peter allowed fear of affliction and ostracism from his community to cause him to deny the very man whose power allowed him to walk on water. Peter is a prime example that fear, if left unharnessed can be very destructive. It prevents us from reaching our full potential in God because fear disables our mobility. Fear disables us from witnessing to our friends and family; it keeps us from taking chances and leaves us with feelings of inferiority, insecurity and inadequacies.

Fear is a detrimental toxin that paralyzes faith and prevents many of us from reaching our ultimate goals in life. We become complacent in our walk with Christ and instead of taking risks, we resort to our world of comfort that seldom incites positive change. Fear in its most progressive form becomes paranoia and we begin to worry about everything, distracting us from our real purpose in life. We worry about losing our homes, our jobs, our marriages and our children. We constantly obsess and worry about our health and appearance. The sad part of this cycle is that when fear is shifted into overdrive, our faith starts to crumble in reverse. The only tool we have against fear is faith, trust and love—gained through a disciplined prayer life. Perfect love, as is indicative of the scripture, casts out all fear.

Even the best amongst us falter at times and fall into the trap of fear. This is why it is absolutely imperative that we develop a prayer life. Throughout this book, you will learn principles on how to rebuild your faith and activate the power within you by beginning or resuming a relationship with Jesus Christ. Remember that God did not give us the spirit of fear. The command to *fear not* is mentioned in the bible 365 times which means that as a believer, we have the opportunity to encourage ourselves each day using references from His word.

In fact, God promised never to abandon nor forget us. God has equipped us with the power and authority to overcome. It is not in His will for believers to walk bombarded with the trials of life. He has given us the power to walk upright with a sound mind, making rational decisions that benefit our lives instead of those that weigh us down.

My sisters and brothers, we will experience tumultuous days but do not be afraid or downhearted as God is with you. Do not be discouraged as only He can help you with things that seem impossible. Remember that even in the word *impossible*, there is a phrase that says I'm Possible! And in everything that you do, do not forget to pray.

Chapter 1

What is Prayer?

*P*rayer is the hinges on which our spiritual doors hang. If there are no hinges, there is no support and therefore no door. Prayer is the edge of protection around us that prevents the devil from doing as he would in our lives. After all, the bible declares in Peter that as believers we must be sober and vigilant because our adversary the devil rages about like a roaring lion seeking whom he may devour. Prayer becomes our weapon of sobriety giving us alms against Satan's attacks even though he is consistently on the prowl.

Prayer is verbal permission permitting God to act on our behalf. It is a weapon that cramps and paralyzes, destroys and kills the orchestrated plans of Satan. In many ways, prayer has transformative properties because the believer does not have to be present in order to see prayer working. I recall the faith of the Centurion as described in the New Testament book of Luke chapter seven where Jesus visited his dwelling:

> "And when he was now not far from the house, the centurion sent his friends to him, saying unto him, Lord, trouble not thyself: for I am not worthy that thou shouldest enter under my roof: Wherefore neither thought I myself worthy to come unto you: but **say** in a word and my servant shall be healed." Luke 7:6-7 (KJV)

1

Here is an example where prayer's transformative powers are in effect because it knows no distance. Once launched, prayer like a missile, heads straight for the intended target. Prayer is also God's way of communing with man. Heart to heart and spirit to spirit. It opens our understanding to the supernatural and miraculous powers of God's unlimited benefits. God calls us friend and will withhold no good things from us. (John 15:14-15)

My friend, pray with great expectations! Prayer is not only meant to break yokes and solve problems but also to heal sickness and pull down strongholds. It enables us to stay plugged into the right power source just like a socket and a plug. Separately, a socket and a plug are useless but once connected, they produce unlimited benefit or danger. So it is when we tap into our God source for power through prayer.

Establishing an effective prayer life requires believers to establish a connection with the one who will be answering those prayers. Prayer acts like a conduit to God, connecting straight to the source. Think of your communication with God as though it was an actual wireless phone service. When one feels the need to connect to a family member or friend they simply pick up their phone and dial a unique number assigned to that person. Depending on the availability of the wireless carrier, a connection is instantly made or the call cannot go through. With God, there is no waiting period or a third party connector to get the believer in direct communication with Him. All God's children has to do is open their mouth and start speaking. Even if their prayers are silent and spoken within the heart, God hears that communication as well. The scriptures remind us in the first chapter of the Old Testament book of Samuel that Eli thought his wife Hannah had been drinking because while she prayed, her lips moved but her voice was not heard. Like Hannah, when our unspoken prayers are rendered from the heart, God interprets the inaudible sounds of our prayers and moves on our behalf. God recognizes our unique calling needs: He knows specifically when you are reaching out to Him and supplies your individual needs accordingly.

Have you ever been engaged in a conversation with someone, whether in person or by phone but could not get a word in because they continuously spoke without listening? Or when they did allow for you to speak, they kept interjecting with their opinions? At some point, you probably felt frustrated and annoyed at their inconsideration or lack of manners. Unfortunately, this is how we treat God sometimes in our own prayer relationship with Him. Prayer is not a monologue but a personal dialogue between you and your Savior so when you pray, you must then listen and wait for God to answer or give instructions. We might take into consideration that this is perhaps the reason why we have one mouth and two ears so that we can speak less and listen twice as much. Ecclesiastes 5:2 encourages us to "let our words be few." The New International Version translates the same scripture warning us not to be too eager to speak in the presence of God.

> "Do not be quick with your mouth; do not be hasty in your heart to utter anything before God. God is in heaven and you are on earth, so let your words be few." ^{Eccl 5:2} (NIV)

When we kneel to pray, we are often guilty of coming before the Lord with a long list of wants. We start with our begging rituals of "Lord give me this" or "I need this from you Jesus" or we beseech God, "When, Where, Why, How" expecting immediate results without pausing or taking the time to linger in His presence to get an answer. God may have given you an answer of Yes or No or He might have said to wait for three months to elapse. But because we are usually in such a hurry, we do not wait long enough for the direction God is giving us and then we subsequently get upset with Him because we believe He has not answered. It is my strong opinion that no one speaks to God without getting an answer. We must ask ourselves these pertinent questions:

1.) When I pray, do I stay still in His presence long enough to hear what He has to say?
2.) Do I pretend that I did not hear Him because He did not give the answer I want?
3.) Was the answer to my question simply an instruction to WAIT?

Do not approach God with hasty rituals expecting immediate resolutions or you will certainly be disappointed. You must wait on God to say yes, no or wait. The amount of time you spend praying is also of little significance to the Lord. Even if you only have time enough to say a prayer in five minutes, it's the sincerity and faith of your prayer that will yield results not the elapsed time of your begging regimen or extended eloquence of speech.

You can spend three minutes in God's presence and it amounts to quality time well spent or you can linger for two or more consecutive hours praying and still not enter into His presence. What makes the difference in your praying time with the Lord is your direct focus on Him. Were you distracted by your current situation or wondering how you were going to make it financially? Was your mind somewhat carried away on the number of phone calls you are to return or did your mind drift on what your child will be eating for dinner? Whatever the thought that shifted your focus from the Lord will also hinder you from being totally surrendered to His presence. Whenever you call on God, do it whole-heartedly and with expectancy.

Unlike our earthly wireless phones, God has a calling system that is never out of range. He will never lose your signal or drop your call. He will never tell you that His battery has to be charged for the conversation to continue nor will you ever call on the Lord and receive his voicemail. The hope that believers have in Jesus Christ is that we can call on Him at anytime and expect to find Him ready to heed our cries. Because He is not on vacation or has a return receipt that He is out of the office. "Behold, He that keepeth Israel [his people] shall neither slumber nor sleep." Psalm 121:4.

Once we are certain that we are focusing our prayers towards the Lord and our hearts and minds are fully concentrated on Him, then prayer will elevate us to the next level in God so we can have a more intimate relationship with Him. It is at this stage that we can gain higher heights in Him and the flow of the anointing gives us revelation. When we pray in this stage, the impossible becomes possible and the unchangeable is forced to change. The broken is restored and things that are dormant in one's life will now come alive. Prayer is food for the hungry and water for the thirsty. It serves as medication to remedy a broken and depressed heart. It is a lifeline to those drowning and a lifeboat to those who are in need of rescue. Prayer is the key to open every closed door and the light that penetrates the darkest darkness. It lifts the spirit and uplifts the soul. Prayer has the power to activate earthquakes that release prison doors and set captives free. Prayer can set any person, bound or restrained, free.

Many people say they do not know how to pray but there is no algebraic formula or scientific theory on the best formats for praying. Prayer is the believer's own simple words to their father. Once comfortable with offering up those simple sacrificial heart-felt words, then the individual find him or herself taking on a sense of confident boldness that comes without trepidation. There is absolutely no language barrier with God so once a believer starts talking, God will understand.

Dr. Martin Luther King Jr. once said, "none can believe how powerful prayer is and what it is able to effect, only those who learned it by experience." I stand in agreement and urge believers once again to fear not because there is still power in prayer.

Prayer Page

Dear sovereign God, here I am before you empty and broken. Cleanse me from within Lord and please pick up my broken pieces and put them together again. Make me whole Lord so I can be a usable vessel for your word. Father I thought prayer was a form of art that I had not learned but I discovered that it is a simple conversation with you. Instill in me oh God how to be still and listen and how to stay in your presence to hear your gentle voice. Father, teach me how to distinguish your voice from those of others and to hear your instructions clearly. In Jesus, name Amen.

"A prayerful life is a powerful life.
A prayer-less life is a powerless life."

Chapter 2

Why Should We Pray?

Many born again Christians lack the understanding of what it means to render effective fervent prayer. Praying in itself is not difficult but effective praying can become challenging if self is not first surrendered. Many believers think we should only pray during a crisis or when we are in need of something; physical or material, which is absolutely furthest from the truth. Matthew 6:33 reminds us to:

> "Seek ye first the kingdom of God, and his righteousness and all these things shall be added unto you." ^{Matt 6:33} (KJV)

In other words, believers should not wait until they are in need to seek the Lord but they should foster a relationship with Him beforehand so that in the midst of turmoil they can rest assure that God already knows what needs to supply and will faithfully supply it even before a request is made. There is an old proverb that says to seek a friend before a friend is needed and indeed its moral applies here. God is looking to commune with his people, to hear from them and fellowship with them on a daily basis as would be common in any earthly relationship. The difference is that God is a supreme being and we worship Him in spirit and in truth so naturally He is not beside us physically in flesh but to those who believe, He is with us supernaturally in the Spirit.

How assuring it is to know that a close friend who sticks closer than a brother is always beside us.

Fostering a committed relationship with the Lord is not always an easy task given the demands of our daily lives. Just as with any other relationship, commitment between two people takes work and sacrifice to build a strong and long lasting union. The same is true in our relationships with God. Since we already know that God made the ultimate sacrifice on the cross through the death of His son Jesus Christ, the rest is up to us as believers. God is always willing and ready waiting. We are usually the problem as we get in our own way then we turn around and say we are waiting on the Lord. We are never waiting on the Lord: God is waiting on us. As Matthew 26 reminds us that the flesh is indeed weak so we must watch and pray so that we do not enter into temptation.

> "Watch and pray that ye enter not into temptation: the spirit indeed is willing, but the flesh is weak." Matt 26:41

The flesh according to Matthew is weak and in need of much restraint. Flesh has no good behavior and it cannot be trusted. It respects no one and is seemingly always getting into and creating trouble. The flesh, as we know, never ceases to war against the spirit. This is one of the reasons why we should pray so that the spiritual man can be fed. Once our spiritual man is equipped with the right tools we can defeat the works of the flesh. We should also be aware that disobedience and pride feeds the flesh. If we nurture and feed our spiritual man then the spirit within us will be stronger. On the contrary, if we feed our flesh it will become stronger and dominate. In physical terms, it is known that we are what we eat. Our physical body is a direct reflection of what it is fed; whether we are over or under weight, nourished or mal-nourished or even if we are highly energized or sluggish. So is our spiritual man a reflection of our prayer life. Our attitudes, language, how we walk and how we handle problems amidst chaos are all results of what we feed our inner spirit.

We learned in the last chapter that there are no special formulas or qualifications necessary to come before the Lord in prayer. A college degree or high school diploma is also not necessary in qualifying a believer to make his or her requests known unto God. However, I like to prompt individuals in gaining what I consider to be a mandatory B.A. status or "Born Again" attitude. In a world where hierarchy and rank gives clout to a select few, we are fortunate as born again Christians to enter into the presence of God without having been born to a royal background. We may not know the Queen's English in its entirety but as children of God, we are bred into a royal priesthood by virtue of our acceptance of Jesus Christ as Lord and Savior. Hence we know the king's language which qualifies us to talk to God as heirs. As His followers then, we should model our lives after His actions and examples. Jesus prayed many times per day, for others as well as for himself. We should do the same.

To illustrate the example of a Christians' necessity to have prayer within their arsenal, I will ask you to stop and if possible get a ripe banana. Take a good look at the fruit you are holding. Next, peel the fruit and lay the skin aside for further analysis later. Go ahead and eat the banana, if you wish, and continue to read this chapter in its entirety. After you have finished with the chapter, go back and take a look at the banana skin that you laid aside. If the illustration worked correctly, you will see that the inside of the banana peel has now turned an unattractive dark brown color. This is because the fruit, while enclosed in the skin brought life and oxygen. Once the fruit is removed, the skin becomes soft and droopy and eventually turns black. In this state, the peel is no longer necessary and its intended purpose is lost so it is fitting to throw the peel away.

Unfortunately like the banana peel, this is exactly what will happen to us if we do not pray or read God's word. Prayer is an essential tool that activates the spirit of the anointing in our lives and provides oxygen and everlasting nourishment to our spiritual growth.

We should not pray to be seen, praised or to be exalted but rather to gain physical and spiritual strength so we may be able to stand against persecution, criticism, discouragement and depression. These are all fiery darts stemming from the plan of the devil. We must pray to first cleanse ourselves so that we rid our lives of negative criticism we cast onto others or the self-righteous attitudes some of us possess. We must pray to release the strongholds that bind us and keep us from growing: Those of grudges and animosity and the spirit of un-forgiveness that paralyze us from the truth.

As followers of Christ, we are constantly in a battle. This battle is a psychological, financial, physical, spiritual and emotional never ending war. No well trained soldier will go to fight a war without being fully equipped with armor and weapons at his disposal. Likewise as Christian soldiers in the army of the Lord, we can be drafted at a moments' notice to fight the many wars that beset us daily. How can we fight a battle ill-prepared? Ephesians chapter 6 says we ought to put on the whole armor of God. Not a portion of the armor lest we get injured in a place we neglected to cover but the entire armor so as to shield us from the fiery darts of the enemy. Let us closely examine the many parts that make up the entire armor.

The helmet of salvation protects our mind from the intrusion of negativity and prevents us from birthing or harboring unwanted evil thoughts. The breastplate of righteousness will prevent our heart and emotions from reacting to hurt from pain inflicted wounds. The belt of truth girds our bowels from parasite and helps us to nurture honesty and integrity. The shoes of peace will allow us to walk through turmoil on the job, easily find a way through chaos at home or misery in the church while still possessing a calm inner spirit. The shield of faith hides the warrior from the fiery darts and arrows of the enemy as he trust in God for deliverance. And, finally, the sword of the spirit, our weapon of protection it cuts on its way in and cuts on its way out. It destroys every illegal power in its path.

> "For we wrestle not against flesh and blood, but against principalities, against powers, against the rulers of the darkness of this world, against spiritual wickedness in high places." Eph 6:12 (KJV)

Paul is reminding us that he discovered that his spiritual fight is not against flesh and blood. In fact, he is not fighting per se with an individual but against forces and the powers of darkness that he cannot see with the physical sight. Imagine fighting a battle where you can neither hear nor see your opponent? The battle would automatically be a one-sided defeat. Nonetheless, if we saturate ourselves in prayer, we will be able to press against spiritual wickedness in high places, low places, dry or wet places or in whomever they inhabit themselves seeking prey. Prayer will keep us fully dressed and ready for war at all times. It is our shield and we should never leave home without it as 1 Thessalonians 5:7 commands us to "Pray without ceasing."

Remember when we pray, we activate spiritual authority that pulls down every high thing that exalts itself against the power, knowledge and wisdom of God. The weapons of our warfare are not carnal but mighty through the pulling down of strong holds and bringing into captivity every thought to the obedience of Christ.[2Cor.10:4-5] Our weapons are not physical: they are not machine guns, machetes, knives or bombs. The weapons that we possess as Christians are mighty through prayer. It touches God and in turn reaches and pulls down and destroys everything that has a stronghold on our lives.

In all our praying, remember that our number one goal is to surrender the flesh and keep self out. Why should we pray? We should pray for a teachable spirit: a spirit of humility that will allow us to avail ourselves fully to the will of God and listen for His direction.

Remember King Nebuchadnezzar who thought so highly of himself that he built tall statues and likenesses of himself. Perhaps he thought he was invincible because of his many accolades and accomplishments. Like Nebuchadnezzar, we too can fall direly off course if we are not careful. It is human to be prideful and ambitious but too much pride can lead to our own demise if not carefully kept in balance. When we pray for the spirit of humility, we acknowledge that of ourselves we can do nothing, but recognize instead that God is the source.

The bible lets us know that out of the abundance of the heart, the mouth speaks. This simply interprets that whatever we are thinking in our hearts, good or evil will manifest through our language and will come pouring out from our mouth. What goes inside our mouth is usually not the problem but the word which comes directly from out of the mouth is usually coming from the heart. ^{Matt15:11}

The next time you feel as though you have ran out of things to pray about, just take a look at the local evening news. Our prayer missions are never complete. Because we live in a world that is on its way to destruction, we must always be in prayer, whether for ourselves or for those around us. Luke 18:1 commands men to pray and not faint. We should pray that our earthly affairs are prioritized and conceived from a heart of love. We should pray for the renewal of our minds that our daily lives are rid of deceit, wickedness, hypocrisies and vindictive attitudes. We should pray that we are not easily enticed or drawn in by worldly pleasures. We should pray for the salvation of our children, family, friends and even the governing legislative bodies that preside over our earthly constitutions. We should continue to pray for those who are bound by witchcraft, drugs, alcohol and sexual immorality; those who are oppressed with infirmities and the medical teams that tend to them tirelessly. We must pray for our missionaries, evangelists and co-workers in Christ and we must never cease to pray for our churches and their leaders who are under constant attack from the enemy.

With such an exhaustive list, our prayer lives are ongoing and we are to continue praying for those around us. Being mindful that we must not be selfish praying only for ourselves or our benefit.

What Happens When We Pray?

> "If my people, which are called by my name, shall humble themselves, and pray, and seek my face, and turn from their wicked ways; then will I hear from heaven, and will forgive their sin, and will heal their land."^{2Chron7:14} (KJV)

This scripture applies a conditional theory in order for it to be effective. God's message is two-fold. There is instruction of what the believer must do in order for God to then do what He promises. The conditional words are *"If"* and *"Then."* In other words, God is waiting to see "if" we will turn from our wickedness in order to "then" deliver on His promise to forgive us and heal our land. Another important command in this verse is to *"turn,"* an active must on the part of the believer. No matter how many mighty works we profess to have done or how many days we spend in fasting or how many acts of benevolence we render, if we do not quit do what is wrong and our behavior aligned with the will of God, our prayers are in vain.

Fear not there is still power in prayer!

Prayer Page

Sweet Jesus, all this time I have been thinking that prayer is for special occasions. But now that my understanding and knowledge is open, teach me how to pray effectively and how to pray in your will. Father let prayer be a part of my daily routine. Help me to make it my first priority and the first thing I do when I open my eyes in the morning. Lord, as of today, I will make sure that wherever I am going, whatever I am planning to do or say I will seek your permission through prayer and never quit or get weary. In Jesus name Amen.

"Come now, and let us reason together, saith the Lord: though your sins be as scarlet, they shall be as white as snow; though they be red like crimson, they shall be as wool." Isaiah 1:18

Chapter 3

When Should We Pray?

Praying always with all prayer and supplication in the
Spirit, and watching thereunto with all perseverance and
supplication of all Saints. ^{Eph 6:18 (KJV)}

There is never a more demanding time for prayer than now. For
this, we ought always to pray. Even before our eyes open to
face the day and before our feet touch the ground, we must
begin our day with an attitude of gratitude, thanksgiving and adoration.
Before we begin our daily tasks or become anxious about the many
follow-ups for the day, we should pay homage to the Lord for keeping
us safely throughout the night and allowing us to awake to face a new
dawn.

Before we start to answer any phone calls, check our voice mail, text
messages, or missed calls, it is imperative that we invite the Holy Spirit
to be in control of us and the course of our day. Do not forget that the
enemy's strategy is to often shift our focus to keep us from praying.
Distractions from voice mails and text messages can unveil a number
of unpleasant situations which could start us in an uproar before we
even have time to consult the Lord. And any number of attacks could
lay wait believers in their voice mail messages alone. By activating the
authority of the Holy Ghost through prayer, believers can rest assure
that they will be equipped to handle any problem or at best ignore any
alarms that would normally cause upset.

Another goal of the devil is to implant fear and doubt in our minds before we even get out of bed. Once we are trapped in that snare, it becomes very challenging to make it through the day as we are lacking in resistance, which I like to refer to as vitamin "R." When we give the first fruit of our existence to something or someone else other than to the Lord in the mornings, we wrestle for the rest of the day to get into the presence of God. This is because we placed God on the back burner from the start.

Prayer is not dependent upon time. In fact believers can utter a word of prayer anywhere and in any situation. We can pray while we are in the shower or even while getting dressed in the morning. During breakfast, we can offer up intercessory prayer on behalf of someone. Remember we are the instruments that God created to free those living in bondage and according to Isaiah 61:1 "The Spirit of the Lord God is upon me; because the Lord hath anointed me to preach good tidings unto the meek; he hath sent me to bind up the brokenhearted, to proclaim liberty to the captives, and the opening of the prison to them that are bound." (KJV)

Even though there is no set time to pray, I encourage believers to set up a prayer schedule. This is more for us to keep committed to the task of praying since there are countless other distractions vying for our attention during the course of the day. Keeping a prayer schedule allows us to stay focused and committed to our prayer goals. I personally like to offer up small prayers for every quarter of time that passes on my watch. So at noon, I know I should be sending up a word of thanks to the Lord. Then again at three in the afternoon I resume my prayers and again at six and nine p.m. Of course, I can pray at anytime but my commitment is to hold myself accountable to those hours so I can offer up some kind of thanks or seek direction from the Lord.

The hours between midnight and 6 a.m. are considered to be hours of warfare. Have you ever noticed that sometimes the most grueling attacks happen just before dawn or are usually late in the nighttime hours when the world is presumably at rest? This is because the enemy tends to strike while believers are sleeping. Sometimes we might awaken at 2:30 a.m. and believe we are suffering from insomnia when in fact the Holy Spirit is awaking us to pray. Mathew 13:25 states that: "While men slept, his enemy came and sowed tares among the wheat, and went his way." (KJV)

God is alerting us that we become prime targets for the enemy while our guards are down and we are relaxed in our comfort zone. This is when the pestilence by nightfall creeps in to enclose around us. The terror that walks in darkness orchestrate attacks on the believer so that by morning, we are saddened with news of death, accidents, contentions, heated arguments, confusion and a number of other plights. Have you ever gotten up in the morning and feel angry with your spouse, children or co-worker and have no real reason for the cause of your frustration? This is because while you were physically sleeping, the enemy took counsel to dictate how he wants your day to unfold, usually allowing confusion of your mind and anger in your spirit.

Do not take it lightly and believe that you are just having a bad day. Yes, your day may have been infused with chaos from the beginning but the plot of the enemy is to use ordinary circumstances and turn them into extraordinary battles. This is why it is so crucial to communicate with the Lord first so He can direct your path. At the very least, talking to God first will enable you to cancel that which was orchestrated in the spiritual realm and allow you to pull down strongholds. The enemy uses every opportunity to work against us therefore we cannot fold our arms and retreat into complacency, we must also pray in every chance. You do not have to kneel down, shout or speak in tongues at every prayer session, you can pray while you are walking to the restroom, prepping for lunch, or even concentrating on an assignment. You can certainly take a minute and send up a quick word of prayer. The Lord understands and will immediately act on your behalf because He sees that you are faithfully committed to prayer.

Prayer can also be non-verbal communication. Praying continually keeps our mind focused on the Lord and the ways of the Lord. It also keeps us in His presence where there is fullness of joy. And staying in God's presence is the safest way to avoid the plots of the enemy. No blue print from Satan drawn against the child of God shall ever come to maturity and no weapon formed will ever prosper. In fact, with your own eyes, you will witness the enemy falling by the thousands. And even when those surrounding you fall by the numbers, none shall touch you because you have placed God at the forefront. He is at your right hand and you shall not be moved.

> [Rejoice] in hope; patient in tribulation; continuing instant in prayer. Rom 12:12 KJV

Paul is exhorting believers that even though we do not see what we often pray for, we have a hope to remain joyful and to rejoice in expectation that it will come to pass. In spite of the tests and the heartaches we must continuously be in prayer while we are plugging through the turmoil. Acts 6:4 says but we will give ourselves continually to prayer, and to the ministry of the word. One songwriter says, "troublesome times are here filling men's heart with fear." Freedom we once knew is being altered in staggering forms. Freedom of speech is limited; government tampers with the public's freedom of religion and our freedom of choice seem obsolete. Things we once held dear and meaningful are now in question. Now is the time to pray.

Luke 6:12 says, "And it came to pass in those days, that he went out into a mountain to pray, and continued all night in prayer to God." Even Jesus prayed all night! Because, as mentioned before, it is in the night season that the powers of darkness prowl and become stronger. The wicked tend to be more rampant with evil intentions during the night. They cannot be easily identified so their wicked works become intensified in darkness. While Satan is scheming, Jesus is cancelling his plots through our prayers. We must pray often to pattern our prayer lives in the same fashion as Jesus.

I encourage you to make the sacrifice to set out on an all-night prayer meeting at church or in your home with other believers as often as possible. If not with other brothers and sisters then do it yourself and make the sacrifice at least one night per week to stay awake and counteract the counsel of Satan and his agents. Once per month or once per year is not sufficient. As is evident by the news of the day, there is trouble everyday and everywhere. How can we circumvent the plans of the enemy when he is on full duty twenty four hours per day and we only pray once per week or per month? The balance would be way off kilter. I urge you as believers to give prayer its proper honor and place in your life. Perhaps you can start by making a conscious effort to retreat to bed early one evening and awake before midnight to prep yourself for a night of praying. At first you might want to pray from midnight to three in the morning and then gradually work your way up to praying until six a.m. Remember our goal is to pray as often as possible, as 1 Peter 4:7 says "but the end of all things is at hand: be ye therefore sober, and watch unto prayer."

As Christians, we do not have to search far and wide to know that the end is near. You can take a glimpse right into your own life, into your church, into your community and notice that it is obvious that we are living in end times. Many have said that their grandparents and great grandparents heard that Jesus is coming soon and still He has not arrived. Therefore the belief is that there is no truth in His return. The truth is that even in Peter's day, believers thought that the return of Christ was a hoax. But he still urges us to be sober minded, conscious of our surroundings and to be vigilant while we watch and pray.

2 Peter 3: 3-4 & 9-10

> ³Knowing this first, that there shall come in the last days scoffers, walking after their own lusts.

> ⁴And saying, where is the promise of his coming? For since the fathers fell asleep, all things continue as they were from the beginning of the creation.

> ⁹The Lord is not slack concerning his promise, as some men count slackness; but is long-suffering to us ward, not willing that any should perish, but that all should, come to repentance.

[10]But the day of the Lord will come as a thief in the night; in the which the heavens shall pass away with a great noise, and the elements shall melt with fervent heat, the earth also and the works that are therein shall be burned up. (KJV)

My brothers and sisters, God is a merciful, caring and compassionate God. He does not want any of us to spend eternity in torment and damnation. As verse 9 points out, God is patient in allowing us time to repent and to build a relationship with Him. Among many of His great attributes are longsuffering and He would not want to see us perish but that all should come to repentance. Eventually however, patience runs out and the time of judgment and accountability lies with us. God is getting to that place of frustration with His children because the more He pardons, the more we sin. These are the days that our prayers need great intensity to help us with this inner man. The world as we know it is fast coming to an end. Where will you spend eternity?

Fear not! There is still power in prayer.

Prayer Page

Heavenly Father, loving master; Indeed you are God and we thank you for your mercy, we thank you for your grace, we thank you for your love. Lord, the question was asked, when should we pray? Father God it is obvious that we do not need binoculars or x-ray vision to see that we ought to pray now and with every opportunity. Help us to be conscious and alert. Also help us to be aware God that your second coming is closer than we believe.

Father, please help us to recognize the importance of praying so that we will not become slack in our commitment to pray. Help us once again to find our position in you and to get back into your secret place. Hallelujah! Glory to God! Thank you Jesus! Holy Ghost, help us to learn from the men of old who spent quality time in your presence, who prayed night and day to touch your heart. Total surrender of my mind and spirit I bring to you. Lord, thank you for your word that has come to shed light in my life. In Jesus name Amen.

"Continue in prayer, and watch in the same with thanksgiving."

Colossians 4:2

Chapter 4

How Should We Pray?

"And it came to pass, that as he (Jesus) was praying in a certain place, when he ceased, one of his disciples said unto him, Lord, teach us how to pray as John also taught his disciples." Luke 11:1

*a*fter carefully listening to their Master praying, the disciples became eager to know how they too can be as effective and fluent in prayer. With that quest for knowledge, they asked of Jesus, "Lord teach us how to pray." We do not know much about the standards that governed their prayers in that time but one can imagine that most of their examples were from religious sects who tended to be ritualistic or repetitive in their prayer. The disciples had now discovered that individual prayer can have its own unique format specific to the experience of the person praying. Jesus responded by saying this is how you should pray:

Our father which art in heaven, Hallowed be thy name.
Thy Kingdom Come, Thy will be done in earth, as it is
    in heaven.
Give us this day our daily bread.
And forgive us our debts, as we forgive our debtors.
And lead us not into temptation, but deliver us from evil:
For thine is the kingdom, and the power, and the glory,
    forever. Amen. Matt 6:9-13 (KJV)

The prayer Jesus taught his disciples was just a mere example in demonstrating the fundamentals of praying. In other words, this is not the only way to pray and it certainly isn't the only words to use in order to be effective. Jesus provided a guide for his disciples to make reference. He says when we enter into His presence we must first recognize that He is the omnipotent God, the creator and ruler of the universe. We must acknowledge his divinity and honor him with our heart for his creativity and his mercies which are renewed and restored in our lives by the second. Through that same model of prayer, Jesus also taught us how to give God permission to establish his will in our lives to fulfill our purpose on Earth. He also wants us to acknowledge that we are sinners who have all sinned and fallen short of His glory. We are imperfect beings in need of forgiveness for our multiple faults. Therefore, we too should be lenient and forgiving with others when they have wronged us.

Another point Jesus made is that we must seek His direction so that we avoid doing evil things. We should embrace Him as our only source of deliverance from every wicked and deadly trap the enemy sets. Most importantly, if we believe that God is an all-knowing omniscient God, then we will not worry about what we cannot see or change but rather trust Him for our daily necessities. Moreover, with great expectancy, wait for Him to perform his duties and fulfill His promises in our lives.

For these reasons I am convinced that there is truly an effective technique in praying. The disciples sought to learn it and Jesus sought to teach it.

How should we pray? We should pray with our mouths open allowing our voice to be heard from words flowing from our inner man into the atmosphere. Spoken words can give and take lives. Words spoken into one's life can be a hindrance or a help to the individuals destiny. Too many times I hear believers say they get confused from praying aloud or that they feel better praying silently within themselves. Some say they get distracted or they are uncomfortable praying aloud around others or that they do not know how to pray. The devil is indeed a liar.

Why is it that we get confused when we pray aloud when we have no problems keeping our daily conversations clear? Often, at prayer times, we get sleepy or confused or afraid that someone may hear us praying. It seems that when we are doing the things of God, that's when we stop to rationalize, pondering whether or not we will offend anyone. As believers, we are often caught in a war between God and Satan fighting for our souls. So instead of praying or reading the word, we feel sleepy, heavy or restless and often put it aside for the next day which is exactly what the devil wants. Satan wants to rob us of our intimacy with the Lord. He often makes our lives miserable or puts trouble in our path so that we become more focused on the situation than to stay in the presence of the Lord and pray. Remember that only God can hear and understand us when we pray within our minds. Satan cannot interpret the prayers of your heart; he can only hear when you open your mouth to bind up his tactics and powers. He understands and responds to your spoken words.

Even though Satan responds to spoken words, bear in mind that it is not just any set of words. For years, I have heard Christians say "Satan I bind you in the name of Jesus Christ and I command you to take your flight back to the pit." Yet Satan is still loose and rampant. For one, Satan is not yet occupying the pit as evidenced by the first three verses in Revelations chapter 20. It is my opinion that man cannot just simply bind Satan and keep him bound; otherwise it would have been done already by Paul, Jeremiah or even David. I believe that through prayer, we can only affect the works, plans, plots and powers of the devil. Saying the wrong prayers will cause us not to see results. When we pray we must be specific and pray the written word of God. In so doing, we are guaranteed power that supersedes the power of the enemy according to Luke 10:19 that says, "Behold, I give unto you power to tread on serpents and scorpions, and over all the power of the enemy: and nothing shall by any means hurt you."

Remember that the examples of Jesus were very specific when he was casting out demons. He called them by name; spirit of deafness, spirit of affliction, spirit of infirmity, etc. And that which he did not call by name, He referred to as a fowl spirit. We should pray in the same manner. Pray against the spirit of depression, the spirit of frustration, confusion, oppression and anything that negatively interferes with our lives. Study the word, open your mouth and use it against Satan and his agents.

Many of our loved ones are being punished innocently because they pray the wrong prayers. One of the major problems of today is unidentified spirits. I see this time and time again in examples like that of depression that manifest itself in the natural. Doctors sometimes give a diagnosis of schizophrenia or multiple personalities disorder or even attention deficit disorder. In my estimation, they are all evil spirits that come to destroy the souls they take over. They are demons and prayer is the only remedy.

I do not believe that medication alone can deliver an individual from spiritual warfare. As mentioned before, spiritual warfare cannot be fought with physical weapons. Individuals suffering from demonic possession or infliction must be spiritually delivered. The demons must be rebuked, commanding them to abandon their assignment, loose their stronghold and their works rendered powerless and invalid. Unbelievably, this is the case for many people in the psychiatric ward or mental institution. Those walking the streets aimlessly or eating from garbage cans sometimes can be attributed to witchcraft. Demonic spirits have taken over their mental capacity to dictate and control their lives. Do not be fooled or caught off guard as 2 Corinthians 2:11 warns not to be ignorant to the devils devices.

Satan takes great advantage when we pray the wrong prayers and cannot identify which spirits are in operation. This is why it is important to open our mouths aloud in prayer especially when we are engaged in a spiritual battle. Command each spirit by name and demand that it loose itself from its assignment. You can only demand this authority when you open your mouth. Your mouth is the gun and your words are the bullets. Remember that in the book of Genesis, God commanded that there be light and there was light. His spoken words created the universe and all its contents. After having fasted for forty days and forty nights, Jesus was confronted by Satan in the desert but Jesus open His mouth and quoted the written words, "man shall not live by bread alone" and "thou shalt not tempt the Lord thy God" causing Satan to retreat and flee.

Satan is more knowledgeable than we are, especially within the spiritual realm. Remember that he once stood at the right hand of God in Heaven so he is fully aware of things happening in the spiritual realm and he is certainly aware of the scriptures. He is also aware by what means he can be defeated and by which methods Christians can gain victory. Two of his main goals are to deceive us into believing he is on our side as he did with Eve in the Garden of Eden and second to keep us silent and blinded from the truth. Remaining silent during spiritual warfare is a sign of defeat. We can only persevere with determined consistency to open our mouths and speak. I fully understand that there are times when we feel oppressed or that our prayers are not reaching further than the roof or we pray but our mouths cannot physically open. I too have experienced spiritual drought and famine but I quickly realized that it was a spiritual attack to keep me silent. Though sometimes weak and dehydrated, I find strength in my weakness, scramble to my feet and begin to fight with all my might. As I remember the words of Dr. Michael Frith that "If I don't fight I will be fought," I refuse to allow myself to be victimized. Therefore, you must press against the mountains no matter how rough and tall, press through the fire despite the heat, press against the floods though it may be deep and press your way up from the valley regardless of its depth and debris. Pressing our way helps to strengthen our spiritual muscles.

Much like a physical gym, when you enter, it is with a goal to accomplish success. Sometimes a trainer is there to coach and push you further than you imagined you wanted to go. The equipment is much heavier than you are and a pain-riddled body was not a part of your plan or reason for going to the gym. But with each session, the pain is what actually makes the difference in pushing the muscles from their lethargic condition into action. Then we can slowly start to see the results regardless of the pain. As the songwriter puts it "no pain, no gain" and this is certainly the case for spiritual warfare. Pray your way out of every turbulent situation despite the odds that presents itself. With the same tenacity and persistence we exhibit in going to the gym to lose weight or gain muscle, we must use the same to open our mouth and pray to destroy strongholds.

With strong determination and great expectancy we should pray. Sometimes we find that at the moment we kneel to pray is when feelings of tiredness and confusion overtake us. But even if we have to change positions, it is crucial that we continue to press along to break through the spiritual barriers that the enemy places in front of our prayer sessions. Like a soldier, we might find that we have to employ tactics that were never a part of our training curriculum just to confuse the enemy. So it is in spiritual warfare, the Holy Spirit may prompt us to apply a practice that is not written in the bible. We may have to pace back and forth, clapping our hands while praying at the same time. I strongly believe clapping your hands, summons the attention of Godly angels to defend you and moaning gets the attention of the Holy Spirit who intervenes and interprets on your behalf. As believers, there are times when you need to get off your knees and lay prostrate before God. Whichever tactic you choose for strategic praying, do it with your whole heart, body and soul.

It is certainly easier to watch soap operas or movies or even spend hours in non-productive telephone conversations but the spiritual prayers of saints take time that tolls on our bodies, our emotions and is sometimes not the most entertaining part of our day. But it is a spiritual necessity as the enemy is counting on distracting us with more appealing events so that he can cut into or eliminate our prayer time.

Ponder this: If a teacher and student is in a classroom and the student would like a pen or paper but did not verbally ask the teacher for it, would the teacher automatically read the students mind and bring it to that student? Of course not! If a child is heading for danger and you yell STOP or NO in your mind, would that help the child? The point here is that prayer is a verbal command and it has to be uttered ninety-five percent of the time to be effective. Sure God can read our minds and certainly prayers can be answered without verbally uttering them but there is power in the spoken word. The walls of Jericho did not tumble down because the people silently prayed. The walls were shattered because of the people's obedience to open their mouths and SHOUT.

How should we pray? With a pure repented heart. Only a pure heart is open to receive from God. To ensure purity, I like to apply what I call the R.E.A.C.T.S formula, which means forgetting about our selfish needs, acknowledging God as the only source and allowing Him to have His way in our life.

R= Repentance. You must first acknowledge you are a sinner and need to be cleansed from all bitterness, strife, un-forgiveness hate and unrighteousness.

E= Empty. In order for God to use and fill us with His power and anointing, we have to empty ourselves from deception, hypocrisy, and animosity. God can use only a clean and empty vessel.

A= Adoration. This is the time to tell God how lovable He is, how much He means to you, how close you want to be to Him and how much you adore and appreciate Him.

C= Commune. Communing with God means getting intimate with Him and sharing your innermost thoughts and feelings. Be still and embrace Him.

T= Thanksgiving. Nothing brings down blessings quicker than offering up praises to God. Express gratitude for life. Thank Him for protecting you from deadly accidents, for keeping you sane when you should have been in a mental institution. Thank Him for pulling you out of the enemy's snare and for overturning every guilty verdict handed to you. Most of all thank Him for favor and the people He placed in your life to assist you along your journey.

S= Supplication. Humble yourself before God and pray that He meets your needs and the needs of others. The next time you intend to achieve results from God and get in His presence; be sure to repent, empty yourself, adore him, commune with him, and do not forget to say thanks.

How should we pray? While it is great to pray in group settings or with two or three gathered, sometimes it is necessary to pray alone. There were many times when Jesus left His disciples in the mornings so that He can pray to God the father. Give the Lord His due diligence in your life by spending individual time with Him. Adam walked in the garden *alone* and this is where God communed and fellowshipped with him.

Having alone time with God is vital to our spiritual growth. It allows us to get closer to God and to get to know more of Him and His pathway. You will be able to empty yourself and confess the real you before Him without fear that others may be listening in on your conversation with Him. You can invite Him in the kitchen or living room, in the attic, basement, bath and bedroom. We can even invite Him into our closet where we often hide our dirty secrets. Being alone with God is fulfilling: There is a sense of peace and satisfaction that comfort us and make us not want to leave His presence. God is the only one who can get you to where you need to be, not where you want to be. Praying by yourself definitely gives you an edge; it strengthens you, grows your confidence so that you are able to hear more clearly and be a better listener. It is almost like being trained privately for a public event. But whether you pray personally or collectively, prayer prepares us for effective public worship.

How should we pray? Collectively! Matthew 18:20 says "For where two or three are gathered together in my name, there I am in the midst of them."

United prayers are always necessary; it equips you with boldness, tenacity and provides a source of strength from each individual. Ever notice how Jesus sends his disciples on assignment in pairs of two? One will be able to catch the other if he falls. Even Jesus chose to walk with not one, but twelve disciples. When praying on one accord, the devil will come and try to intercept the weaker vessel but he will always be unsuccessful when there are many joined together fighting. A gang member by himself is usually frail and intimidated but that same member gains significant strength in the presence of his other gang members because now he has the strength of the majority. Why does the same person act differently? Because he knows that by himself he is vulnerable and is likely to be defeated but with his family he is confident because there is strength in numbers and together they become a force.

Prayer Page

Heavenly father you are God, you are the giver of life, you are mighty, you are the King of kings and the Lord of lords, you are awesome. God I want to thank you for being there for me every step of the way in spite of me neglecting you. Lord I thank you for this book that has taught me strategic prayer points on how we should pray. Father let your perfect will be done in my life and let me not walk contrary to righteousness and truth to your word. Lord your word says whatever I bind on earth is bound in heaven and whatever I loose on earth is loose in heaven. In the name of Jesus, I take authority over every power of darkness and I bind up every works of the devil that has been assigned to destroy my life. I render them powerless null and void. With the power invested in me, I confiscate devices set up to be used against me and my family. In Jesus name amen!

One thousand shall flee at the rebuke of one; at the rebuke of five shall he flee; til ye be left as a beacon upon the top of a mountain, and as an ensign on a hill. Isaiah 30:17

Chapter 5

Testimony: Feuding cousins for 10 years!

O n a beautiful moonlit, cool spring night my girlfriend and I were engaged in a phone conversation reminiscing on the awesomeness of God. We exalted God's creativity and basked in His presence and reminded one another of how far the Lord brought us through the power of prayer. She then said to me, "I have two cousins, Tulip and Blossom whom have not spoken to each other in over ten years. The rift between them began over third-party news that had reached back to both cousins. "It pains my heart to see them like this, I wish they would put away the foolishness and act civil with each other," my girlfriend said. Then she asked if I could pray for them on her behalf.

Approximately two to three days later, I wrote their names and laid it before God and began to pray earnestly for them. This was in March of 2003 and there was a seven night revival being hosted by Juanita Bynum in Queens New York. The seven nights that the revival was initially intended turned into seven weeks and I found myself leaving work in the evenings, sometimes without stopping home and heading straight to the event.

On one particular night of the gathering, I went directly home because I was feeling down in spirits and a bit tired. As I lay in bed relaxing, the phone rang and it was my girlfriend calling with excitement in her voice asking me to guess what had taken place. Since I couldn't guess, she continued to gush that Blossom had shown up on Tulip's doorsteps and rang the doorbell. Tulip, after snapping out of the shock of seeing her cousin, asked Blossom what she was doing there. Blossom simply answered, "I'm here to let bygones be bygones and I do not wish to live like this anymore. They embraced each other in tears as Tulip began to lead Blossom and welcome her into the house.

Initially, I could not recall whom she was referring to but as she jogged my memory, I remembered it was the feuding cousins for whom I had prayed. I was in such awe and disbelief all at once. Not because I doubted God's miraculous power but because so little time had elapsed since my prayer and their reunion. Even though I was not feeling well, the excitement of the news urged me out of bed and landed me into church to thank God for His blessings.

It was about 11:30 p.m. I know the revival ended for the evening but each night they would continue at one a.m. in a prayer service to pray for those who hungered and thirst for more of God's righteousness. One of those people going through a drought was me. At the time, I felt as though I was spiritually famished and starving and in much need of feeling closer to the Lord. I hurriedly got dressed and drove approximately four miles to be at the church at one a.m. in the morning. I just could not stay away. I always want to learn more, see more and know more about the heart, mind and ways of the Lord. I now know that God can do anything because I have personally experienced His goodness. Those early morning prayers enabled me to reach a higher level in Jesus Christ. I have a relationship with Him allowing me to spend quality time in His presence and hide in His secret place. It was few months prior to the revival, I had given my life to the Lord, I was not very strong so I was still in disbelief at how quickly God had answered my prayers regarding those feuding cousins.

Although I have witnessed numerous miracles and seen many prayers answered, it was almost as if I did not completely believe. When one is ignorant to the character and attributes of God, he or she minimizes Him to their level not realizing He is an omniscient, omnipotent and omnipresent God. How can human's finite mind fathom an infinite limitless God? We simply cannot. But, seeking more and more of Him daily invites us into His realm where we can experience His awesome wonders. There were times when I would say, God are you really using Jasmine for your purpose? For a brief moment, ignorance made me walk in doubt, talk with fear and embrace unbelief.

I am thankful that God has helped me to experience His glory in ways that now puts doubt far from my thoughts. I later realized that God is no respecter of person or thing. Once we avail ourselves to God, He uses us as vessels for His mission. Remember in the Old Testament book of Numbers chapter 22, God used a donkey to speak to the prophet Balaam and in 1 Kings17, it was a Raven that was used to distribute food to His servant Elijah. These are perfect examples that God has the power to command and subject anything to His obedience to carry out good deeds. It is totally out of the ordinary for humans to consider accepting food from a raven. Ravens are usually thought of as scavengers who roam about the earth eating dead or dirty things. But, God does not show partiality or favoritism in whom or what He will use to carry out His plans. Likewise, if we avail ourselves to the will of God, He will use us just the same if not more.

I must caution you though, as believers willing to be used of God, we must keep ourselves at a certain level. This means we have to close our ears to gossiping and tale bearing. We must also be very careful to whom and what we listen. If we digest toxic information, then naturally we will give off contaminated energy. Sowing seeds of discord is one of six things mentioned in Proverbs 6:16-19 that God strongly hates.

Professing believers must feast on the word of God daily. If we seek the things of God, we will not have space enough to absorb negativity or react unkindly to anyone. The Old Testament book of 1 Chronicles 16:11 persuades us to "Seek the Lord and His strength, [and to] seek his face continually." If our mind is focused on the things of the Lord, then we will seldom pay attention to petty behavior or be concerned with carrying out revenge on anyone that have done us harm. As a matter of fact, once an individual turns his or her focus directly on the ways of the Lord, he or she will not have time to concentrate on grudges, yet alone to hold them. I am not disregarding the magnitude of hurt that others may have inflicted or asking that believers minimize its damage but I am encouraging you to instead channel your hurt onto the Lord and to remain in His presence. Seek God's heart constantly and you will find yourself in his secret place and hidden under his protective barrier. At this point, we will be so consumed with love, gentleness, compassion and meekness that peace will reign in our hearts and free us from the bondage of malice and un-forgiveness. This level of peace with God helps us to understand that whatever pain and hurt we endured was strictly a manifestation of Satan's work. We will learn to see others as God sees us and will easily forgive with a heart of love knowing that the glory goes to God. Fear not, there is still power in prayer.

Prayer Page

Almighty God, creator of all humanity, I ask that your cleansing blood flow through my entire body and purify me. Wash me thoroughly inside out and remove any darkness found within me. Oh keeper of my soul; empty me from all strife, bitterness and malicious will. Take my heart and give me a brand new start. Teach me how to be still, Lord, and arrange my thoughts so that they are more like thee. Father God, help me to close my eyes and ears to anything that is not beneficial to my spirit. Thank you for deliverance. In Jesus name Amen.

Search me, O God, and know my heart: try me, and know my thoughts: And see if there be any wicked way in me, and lead me in the way everlasting. Psalms 139:23-24

Chapter 6

The Night Bird

You will not fear the terror of the night, nor the arrow that flies by day. Psalm 91:5 KJV

a few years ago I went home to Jamaica for a vacation. As always, my father was the first to get out of bed before anyone else in the house. One particular morning, I remember being awakened to the loud sound of him talking to himself. I was too lazy however to get out of bed to see what was going on and sleepily came to the conclusion that it was really nothing serious. When I finally awoke, I asked him why he was making so much noise. His response was that every morning when he opens the door, he sees some white powder-like substance sprinkled at the entrance of the three doorways on the veranda. I asked how long had he noticed this and he said it has been happening for weeks going on months to the best of his remembrance. I stood in shock as I inquired further. He continued that since his wife (my mother) got sick and came back home he has noticed the milky substance directly in front of the three doors. I really did not know what else to say or how to respond since he was the one having to cope with the situation and was convinced of what he had been seeing.

I asked dad if he would allow me to witness for myself the sprinkled powder that constantly appeared at the doorways before he cleans it the next time. Sure enough, the next morning I was frightened out of my sleep to my father's ranting as he yelled my name for me to come quickly. I knew exactly why he was calling and I speedily got out of bed to witness the scene. "What do you say to all these things?" he asked rhetorically. Still venting, he said, "look how far my home is from the main road; I do not interfere with people, yet they leave from wherever they come from to throw white stuff in my place." After examining the area, I did notice the white substance in front of all three doorways. The shocking mystery about this circumstance was that the milky residue; with what seemed like intentional precision was willfully placed in the direct center of all three doors which lead to my mother's bedroom, my father's bedroom and the other to the living room.

I seldom doubt my father but I did begin to wonder about the strangeness of these events that I could hardly understand. To bring some sense to the mystery, I offered dad an explanation that it was not done by human hands and was simply the droppings of some bird. Of course he was not convinced. He adamantly held on to the notion that someone had purposefully sprinkled powder in front of his door and that he was quite aware of these things. Furthermore, he had been experiencing these events for weeks.

I simply told him not to worry and that he will not see it again the next day. In a scolding voice, he said he thinks I am taking his situation for a joke. I reassured him that I was not joking but that the milky substance was merely the doings of a bird. "Birds do not fly at night," he grunted. "Moreover, I am always sitting on the veranda and I make sure it is swept before I turn in to bed and that all the chairs are turned down." After going back and forth for a while, I insisted that he would no longer see the spots as I knew how to pray.

I went back to my room and pondered the events. I did not know for certain that it was a bird that made the white droppings because I had seen the spots after the fact. Originally, I thought he was referring to some sort of powder but the substance looks more like dried milky residue. Nevertheless, I began to pray. If it was a bird, I commanded that its wings be broken and his eyes blinded so he will not see the house anymore. I prayed that if this bird was sent by a person, I ordered it to return to its sender and not to return to this property. I stripped it from its assignment and rendered it powerless in Jesus name.

Approximately 9p.m. that night, the family was sitting on the veranda engaged in conversation. The night was dark but much to my surprise, I saw what looked like a white bird flying at a pointed angle directly towards the veranda in full speed. As if an angel was standing in its way, I witnessed when the bird made a sharp U-turn and started to head in the opposite direction. I am not sure if anyone else saw it as there were no comments but when I saw what happened I smiled to myself and said, "Aha, indeed it is you." Perhaps it was coming to deliver its usual mysterious white package but that night it was disappointed because it was not able to do so. I then asked to be excused from the conversation and returned to my bedroom where I began to pray again. This time, I asked the Lord to cast down and bind up every stronghold and every high thing that exalts itself against the power of God. It has since been six years since that dilemma and until the current day, my father has never complained about another white spot on the veranda again. Fear not, there is still power in prayer.

There shall no evil befall thee, neither shall any plague come nigh thy dwelling. Psalm 91: 10

Prayer Page

Holy Spirit you are welcome in my life. Omnipotent father, how excellent is your name. Father God I exalt your name above all other names; you have been the lifter of my head, my strong tower and my shelter from the arms of the wicked. Lord, you are my body guard and my covering. Heavenly Father I appreciate that you are in control of my life. Lord, I am thankful that you look beyond my faults and see instead, how much I am in need of your grace and mercy. You always come to my rescue and I am grateful beyond words.

Holy Spirit, I thank you for ordering my steps. Lord I want to thank you for hearing and answering my prayers. Thank you for strength to face each day. Lord, I ask you to be all around me that I shall not be moved by any demons or devil. Like the tree planted by the rivers of water I will stand firmly so that I may magnify and exalt your name. Hallelujah! Father God I have tasted and seen your goodness; I have seen the works of your angels that encamp around me to deliver me from the terror by night and the pestilence that walk in the darkness. I give you the glory, the honor and the praise in Jesus mighty name. Amen

Rest in the Lord, and wait patiently for him: fret not thyself because of him who prospereth in his way, because of the man who bringeth wicked devices to pass. Psalm 37:7

Chapter 7

A Faith-full life

a faith-full life is a life that walks about freely with a do-not-care attitude. Simply put, as a Christian you do not care how God is going to do it; you do not care when He is going to do it and you do not care where He is going to perform His blessings.

To live a faith-full life, you must give yourself away by surrendering yourself to the way of God. Most importantly, you cannot allow interference from frustration, disappointment, criticism, chaos and indecision to cause you to worry. One who walks in a faith-full pathway rejoices though there is famine; shout praises though there is no income from being unemployed, worships though there is a pending foreclosure on his or her home and sings as though the storms have no impact on his or her surroundings. It does not matter what is happening, faith makes evident the results of our prayer.

A faith-full life does not react negatively to life's circumstances. Whether it is rejection or a loss of possessions, economic recession or even death, the believer is always prepared for the next mighty move of God and is ready to go to the next level. A life lived in faith is always conscious of whom is the author and finisher of his or her faith and that God is the one who originates and directs your life. He that started a good work in you and for you will and is able to complete it to perfection. You will never be far from God's mind and He will never abandon you. Your needs will be furnished and he will provide all that you may ask or need of Him.

40

A life lived in faith will activate fountains in a wilderness; rivers in the desert. It opens the Red Sea, part the waters of Jordan and slay a giant named Goliath. Furthermore, faith will provide houses you never built and cars you never bought. A faith-full life empower you to keep on going though the journey is tough; to persevere even when you cannot physically see the path nor have knowledge of your destination. It will inspire you to keep on giving of yourself even when there is no returned gratitude or appreciation. And it will allow you to keep on planning even though the results are dissatisfying.

God is pleased with a life that is faith-full and demonstrates belief. Belief is the foundation on which a life filled with faith is built. Matthew 17:14-21 speaks of a man who confronted the disciples because his child was possessed and tormented by demons. This man knew the works and power of Jesus. The man assumed that the disciples, having been followers of Jesus, had the same power as Jesus and should be able to do the things Jesus did by casting the unclean spirit out of his child. The disciples did the opposite of what he expected and when Jesus came, the man complained about his disappointment with the disciples. Jesus then rebuked the demons and immediately the demons left and the child was set free. Astonished, the disciples asked, "Why couldn't we cast out the demons?" Jesus answered, "because of your unbelief." In other words they were faithless. Then He went on to say, if you have faith as a mustard seed you shall say to this mountain (the problem or your situation) remove and it is done. The key verse is Matthew 17:21, which says: [21] "Howbeit this kind goeth not out but by prayer and fasting" (KJV). In other words, this kind of demon will not and cannot leave unless you give yourself over to fasting and prayer.

Romans 12:3 remind us that "God hath given every man a measure of faith." Here Jesus was telling his disciples that if they activate their faith, even if only the size of a grain of sand, they would be amazed at the power which will manifest through them; in such a way that every hindrance, obstacle, or mountain will vanish. Likewise with believers, if it is a financial mountain, a marital issue, or a health concern; whatever the mountain is can only be moved if you believe.

Ponder this thought: We believe that we will see tomorrow so we make all sorts of plans for the day. When we get in our car or public transportation, we are so confident that we will get to our destination safely. We never wonder what if the wheels come off the vehicle or if the engine will collapse or run out of fluids. We ride the elevators with the assurance that we will get off on the tenth floor without plunging to the bottom of the elevator shaft. When flying on the airlines, we call our friends or relatives to tell them what time the flight will arrive. We never think about the plane falling from the skies or other delays; we believe wholeheartedly that we will get to our destination by all means necessary.

Belief is a very important factor in our everyday lives but most importantly in Christendom. We wrap and channel our beliefs around everything else except the most guaranteed which is in the almighty God and His words. Whenever it comes to God and the things of God we begin to reason, rationalize and analyze and waiver.

> For verily I say unto you, That whosoever shall say unto this mountain, Be thou removed, and be thou cast into the sea; and shall not doubt in his heart, but shall believe that those things which he saith shall come to pass; he shall have whatsoever he saith. ^{Mark 11: 23} (KJV)

Once you've declared a statement or a healing by faith, stand firm on that faith and believe that the evidence will immediately follow. Of course the enemy will make sure you believe you are still in bondage or that your symptoms have remained the same. This is what I call temporary residual effects, meaning that since we live in the physical, a natural process must take place. In other words, once you've commanded a faith action, it is not like the cartoons where the action instantaneously takes place magically with a poof of smoke or the sprinkling of fairy dust. Take for example a tooth ache. Having gone to the dentist, the tooth is extracted but for a few days there is still the feeling of pain resembling that of a toothache. Is it the tooth that hurts you? The tooth is gone but what remains afterward might be referred pain or the residual effect of having that tooth removed. In any case, it is only temporary and will not last too much longer. This is medically known as phantom pain.

Yes, your mind will start telling you everything but the truth, which, not surprisingly as humans, we are more inclined to believe. Human beings are visual-based believers. We have to see to believe which is the exact opposite of faith's command to believe without seeing. As a believer, you need to allow the fullness of your faith to speak life and healing. If the pain re-enters, rebuke it and repeat, "I know I am healed in Jesus name". The orchestrated plan of the enemy is to get you to doubt and reverse your own words. If you are still feeling pain and in that split second you say, "Oh boy, this pain is not going anywhere" then immediately you cancel the positive with the negative and replant the seed of sickness once again in your body.

In Luke 17:5, the apostles asked Jesus to increase their faith. Once again, Jesus responded that it is not necessarily an increase in faith that they need, otherwise he would not have made reference to the size of a mustard seed, but what they need to do is to act on the faith they already have, albeit very little. You will be in awe of what you will be able to uproot and discord once your faith is activated. Every mundane or dead situation in your life will bow and obey you.

> And the apostles said unto the Lord, Increase our faith.[6] And the Lord said, If ye had faith as a grain of mustard seed, ye might say unto this sycamine tree, Be thou plucked up by the root, and be thou planted in the sea; and it should obey you. [Luke17:5] (KJV)

With natural eyes, most things seem impossible so we begin to waiver. In the back of our minds we already say, "No I don't think it's going to work." Once the thought crosses your mind, unless you rebuke it, do not bother to pray, because you are already defeated. You cannot pray defeated and expect to be victorious. The first chapter of James says: "But let him ask in faith, nothing wavering. For he that wavereth is like a wave of the sea driven with the wind and tossed.[7] For let not that man think that he shall receive any thing of the Lord. [8] A double minded man is unstable in all his ways. [James1: 6]

The songwriter says to "Turn your eyes upon Jesus and look full in his wonderful face" and start living a life that is full of faith. Friends, you can only inherit a life full of faith through prayer. The more you pray the more comfortable you feel with God. The more comfortable you become, the more you will trust Him and of course, the more you trust Him, the more you believe. Once you believe, your faith is in motion to accomplish its fullness.

In the scripture below, I have underlined key words from the text taken from Matthew 17:20. It is important that believers remind themselves that the power lies within their own hands. I encourage readers to underline the same words in their bibles so it serves as a visual mental note to oneself that faith lies in the believer.

> And Jesus said unto them, because of your **unbelief**: for verily I say unto you; if you **have** faith as a grain of mustard seed you shall **say** unto **this** mountain, **remove**; and nothing shall be impossible unto you. [Matthew 17:20] (KJV)

<u>Unbelief</u>: To waver between two opinions. How do you know unbelief is at work? If you request prayer for a certain situation and you are still asking multiple others to pray about the same thing, that is doubt and unbelief.

<u>Have</u>: That which is in your position: If you use the faith you have by activating power, you are in control of your situation. You do not even have to lay hands, just speak the word and you will see results.

<u>Say</u>: Spoken words; make utterance. The world was created by spoken words. Life and death lies in the power of your tongue. The man with the sick servant told Jesus he did not have to go to the location of the sick for the miracle to be performed. He asked Jesus to just speak the words. Jesus responded that He had never seen such a <u>great faith</u> in Israel."

<u>This</u>: this means the immediate problem at hand; that which stands in the way and posing a threat right now.

<u>Remove</u>: to take away or to move from one location to the next. An object was elsewhere but is now placed in your path to create havoc. With the authority invested in you, you will now speak to that thing, and tell it to go back from whence it came.

If you can speak it, believe it, and leave it, then you will receive it. You will know for sure that nothing is impossible or will be too hard for God to do on your behalf. Live a life that is full of faith (faith-full) and you will be fearless, doubtless, and faithful. Without faith, it is impossible to please God. Fear, doubt, and unbelief are enemies of our soul; they group together to rob us of our inheritance, destroy our potential, kill our destiny and prevent us from reaching our ultimate level in God. You will never see one without the other. Fear, doubt and unbelief are what I call bastard triplets; sent to keep us in bondage. These triplets can hold us hostage and in captivity against our will forever. They can prevent our mind from being transformed and conformed to the characteristics of God. Whatever prevents our mind from being renewed and keeps us distracted from caring about the things of God is bondage. Fear not, there is still power in prayer.

Prayer Page

Heavenly father, you are awesome and wonderful. Forgive me Lord for all my iniquities, every transgression and every impurity. Mighty God teach me how to live a faith-full life and teach me oh God to be of a sound mind so I will not be unstable in my actions. Lord, I am asking you to teach me how to apply belief to my daily living. Father I need to know how to cast the weight of doubt and unbelief from my thoughts. Lord it is my desire to walk in faith. The cares of life seem so much and sometimes keeping faith is very challenging. I know you specialize in things that seem impossible so here I am before you Lord crying out for help.

God I have just read this passage on how to live the faith-full life, a life that is full of faith in you. Lord, no matter what storm I may face, no matter what challenges I may face, I am going to trust you. No matter what fiery furnace I may face or in what lions' den I may be cast, father God, I want to have faith enough to know that you will come to my rescue, like you have done for Paul and Silas, Daniel, and the three Hebrew boys. Father God, I now turn my mind to you, I turn my heart to you, Lord wash me now and give me a spiritual blood transfusion that your blood will continue to flow through my veins. From now on I will live a faith-full life in Jesus name. Amen.

Now faith is the substance of things hoped for, the evidence of things not seen. Hebrews 11:1

Chapter 8

I Know and confess

The format for this chapter is written a little differently because it is intended to inspire any believer to literally open your mouth and confess the word of God in and over your life and the life of your families. Use them to encourage yourself and transform your mind. A positively engaged mind is a productive, happy, peaceful and renewed mind. Not only do I want you to confess these scriptures until you know them but I want you to believe and apply them to your life daily.

So many times I hear people making the mistake of claiming and accepting unpleasant situations in their lives. They do this without consciously realizing that life and death really lies in the power of their tongue. Instead of saying "I have cancer" or claiming "my diabetes," "my asthma," "my migraine or "my pain", start confessing the situation as how you want it to be. Speak those things that are not as though they were or the way you would like them to be. Remember your spoken words are seeds that you are sowing into existence and whatever you sow must grow. Once you confess these words, you are automatically planting seeds which will take root and bring forth results, positive or negative. Empower and educate yourself with the word of God. You will then be equipped to edify others and eradicate every seed, missile, bomb and grenade planted by Satan and his army. Know who and what you are and confess it.

Thou shalt also decree a thing, and it shall be established unto thee: and the light shall shine upon thy ways. [Job22:28] (KJV)

I HAVE REPENTED

Acts 17:30 And the times of this ignorance God winked at; but now commandeth all men every where to repent:

I AM SAVED

Luke 9:56 For the Son of man is not come to destroy men's lives, but to save them. And they went to another village.

Luke 7:50 And he said to the woman, Thy faith hath saved thee; go in peace.

I AM LOVED

John 3:16 For God so loved the world, that he gave his only begotten Son, that whosoever believeth in him should not perish, but have everlasting life.

Revelation 3:19^KJV As many as I love, I rebuke and chasten: be zealous therefore, and repent.

Revelation 3:19^Amplified Those whom I [dearly and tenderly] love, I tell their faults and convict *and* convince *and* reprove and chasten [I discipline and instruct them]. So be enthusiastic *and* in earnest *and* burning with zeal and repent [changing your mind and attitude].

I AM HEARD

Psalm 3:4 I cried unto the Lord with my voice, and he heard me out of his holy hill. Selah

Psalm 118:5 I called upon the Lord in distress: the Lord answered me, and set me in a large place.

I AM DELIVERED

Psalm 34:4 I sought the Lord, and he heard me, and delivered me from all my fears.

Psalm 34:17 The righteous cry, and the Lord heareth, and delivereth them out of all their troubles.

I AM RESCUED

2 Peter 2:9 The Lord knoweth how to deliver the godly out of temptations, and to reserve the unjust unto the day of judgment to be punished:.

I AM STRENGTHENED

2Corinthians 12:9 And he said unto me, My grace is sufficient for thee: for my strength is made perfect in weakness. Most gladly therefore will I rather glory in my infirmities, that the power of Christ may rest upon me.

I AM CHOSEN

John 15:16 Ye have not chosen me, but I have chosen you, and ordained you, that ye should go and bring forth fruit, and that your fruit should remain: that whatsoever ye shall ask of the Father in my name, he may give it you.

Ephesians 1:4 According as he hath chosen us in him before the foundation of the world, that we should be holy and without blame before him in love:

I AM ADOPTED

Eph 1:5 Having predestinated us unto the adoption of children by Jesus Christ to himself, according to the good pleasure of his will,

I AM ACCEPTED

Eph 1:6 To the praise of the glory of his grace, wherein he hath made us accepted in the beloved.

I AM REDEEMED

Eph 1:7 In whom we have redemption through his blood, the forgiveness of sins, according to the riches of his grace;

I AM ENLIGHTENED

Eph 1:9 Having made known unto us the mystery of his will, according to his good pleasure which he hath purposed in himself:

I HAVE POWER

Luke 10:17 And the seventy returned again with joy, saying, Lord, even the devils are subject unto us through thy name.

Luke 10:19[KJV] Behold, I give unto you power to tread on serpents and scorpions, and over all the power of the enemy: and nothing shall by any means hurt you.

Deuteronomy 8: 18 [KJV] But thou shalt remember the Lord thy God: for it is he that giveth thee power to get wealth, that he may establish his covenant which he sware unto thy fathers, as it is this day.

I AM SUSTAINED

Psalm 3:5 I laid me down and slept; I awaked; for the Lord sustained me.

I AM BLESSED

Luke 6:22 Blessed are ye, when men shall hate you, and when they shall separate you from their company, and shall reproach you, and cast out your name as evil, for the Son of man's sake.

I AM PROTECTED

Isaiah 43:2 When thou passest through the waters, I will be with thee; and through the rivers, they shall not overflow thee: when thou walkest through the fire, thou shalt not be burned; neither shall the flame kindle upon thee.

Psalm 32:8 I will instruct thee and teach thee in the way which thou shalt go: I will guide thee with mine eye.

I AM KEPT

Deuteronomy 1:31 And in the wilderness, where thou hast seen how that the Lord thy God bare thee, as a man doth bear his son, in all the way that ye went, until ye came into this place.

Psalm 30:3 O Lord, thou hast brought up my soul from the grave: thou hast kept me alive, that I should not go down to the pit.

I AM FEARLESS

Isaiah 41:13 For I the Lord thy God will hold thy right hand, saying unto thee, Fear not; I will help thee.

Psalms 118:6 The Lord is on my side; I will not fear: what can man do unto me?

I AM WAITING

Psalm 27:14 Wait on the Lord: be of good courage, and he shall strengthen thine heart: wait, I say, on the Lord.

I AM HEALED

Malachi 4:2: But unto you that fear my name shall the Sun of righteousness arise with healing in his wings; and ye shall go forth, and grow up as calves of the stall.

Psalm 30:2 O Lord my God, I cried unto thee, and thou hast healed me.

I AM VICTORIOUS

2 Corinthians 2:14 Now thanks be unto God, which always causeth us to triumph in Christ, and maketh manifest the savour of his knowledge by us in every place.

Romans 8:37 Nay, in all these things we are more than conquerors through him that loved us.

I AM KNOWLEDGEABLE

Philippians 3:8 Yea doubtless, and I count all things but loss for the excellency of the knowledge of Christ Jesus my Lord: for whom I have suffered the loss of all things, and do count them but dung, that I may win Christ.

I HAVE AUTHORITY

Luke 10:19^{Amplified} Behold! I have given you authority and power to trample upon serpents and scorpions, and [physical and mental strength and ability] over all the power that the enemy [possesses]; and nothing shall in any way harm you

I AM REWARDED

Isaiah 1:19 If ye be willing and obedient, ye shall eat the good of the land:

Psalm 19:11 Moreover by them is thy servant warned: and in keeping of them there is great reward.

I AM HAPPY

Matthew 6:25 Therefore I say unto you, Take no thought for your life, what ye shall eat, or what ye shall drink; nor yet for your body, what ye shall put on. Is not the life more than meat, and the body than raiment?

Philippians 4:11 Not that I speak in respect of want: for I have learned, in whatsoever state I am, therewith to be content.

Psalm 30:11 Thou hast turned for me my mourning into dancing: thou hast put off my sackcloth, and girded me with gladness;

I HAVE GODLY WISDOM

James 3:17 But the wisdom that is from above is first pure, then peaceable, gentle, and easy to be intreated, full of mercy and good fruits, without partiality, and without hypocrisy.

I HAVE UNDERSTANDING

Proverbs 3:4 So shalt thou find favour and good understanding in the sight of God and man.

I WILL INHERIT ETERNAL LIFE

Revelations 21:7 He that overcometh shall inherit all things; and I will be his God, and he shall be my son.

Matthew 5:5 Blessed are the meek: for they shall inherit the earth

Prayer Page

God, I am guilty of neglecting you many times. Help me to know thy truth and to confess them from my mouth. Give me strength to utilize your word everyday and to know that you have given me power within my tongue to speak life to my circumstances. Forgive me for the sins of omission and those sins that are willfully committed. Help me to walk in the paths of righteousness that I may not walk contrary to your command. Let your perfect will take pre-eminence in my life. Father God your word says, whatever I bind on earth is bound in heaven and whatever I loose in heaven is loose on earth. With that authority; I bind the spirit of prayerlessness, I bind the fowl spirit that tries to keep us silent and ignorant to the truth of God. I bind every deceptive spirit and cast them out into outer darkness. I now loose the power of prayer, boldness, praise and worship in my environment. In Jesus name Amen.

Chapter 9

The Misconception of
Praise & Worship

*W*hat is praise? How do we praise? Why should we praise? Praise and worship is one of the most powerful weapon believers have in their possession. As such, we should never allow it to escape our presence. Sincere praise will lead into worship that when conducted in the correct way, is like a bulldozer plowing down the mountainside. Nothing can stand in the way of real praise and worship when done in spirit and in truth. Worship destroy yokes, lighten burdens, and strangle spirits of depression and heaviness allowing the atmosphere to be conducive for joy and peace. Praise and worship is the master key to open the heart of God. It is also the spiritual energy that precedes an anointed, power-packed Holy Ghost filled church service. I believe praise is the pipeline through which worship runs and the faucet through which the anointing flows. The presence of God lingers in a place where true praise and worship takes preeminence over program and ritualistic services. As you continue to explore the pages of this chapter, you will see how praise and worship moves God to intervene for His people.

From observation, I notice that praise and worship often takes on a traditional ritual. Sunday after Sunday or Sabbath after Sabbath, believers go through the same motion that is expected of them sometimes without enjoying the liberty of praise. It usually starts with

56

the praise and worship team. Whether through song, prayer or music, their role is to usher in the presence of the Holy Spirit. The Holy Spirit destroys yokes in the atmosphere so believers can worship and free themselves. Instead, what often takes place is a butchering ceremony, where the intended praise is embalmed by the members and then buried in the grave by the pastor. The analogy is a bit extreme, I know, but this burial session of dead praise is exactly what is happening during praise and worship. We do not serve a dead God so why would we offer Him dead praises? Praise and worship is a reverencing act; filled with adoration and thanksgiving. It is a time of surrendering and listening and waiting upon the Lord. It certainly should not take on a ritual of rushing through as many songs as possible before the fifteen minute time slot allotted to praise and worship is expired. Sometimes it is most effective to just linger in the spirit while concentrating on the words of one song. This allows the anointing of God to flow which breaks up strongholds in the atmosphere.

Shortly after praise and worship there should be a period of meditation or stillness to hear God's direction for the duration of the service. This moment of waiting is often intercepted by a well organized program dictating the order of service. Paul wrote to the Corinthians to "let all things be done decently and in order" but there is a difference with conducting the service in order and in limiting the flow of the anointing to a specific timeslot. This effected routine is so typical in churches that Christians can almost recite what is to take place in a given service. I see it happen all the time. The services are called to order with opening prayer and a hymn, then the praise and worship team tries to usher in the presence of God with a few choruses. This is typically followed by a song, scripture reading and the collecting of the tithes and offering. After this, the keynote speaker or pastor is introduced and more time is spent announcing his credentials (Evangelist, Bishop, Doctor of Divinity, etc.) than actually getting into the word. By the time he gets to about fifteen minutes into his sermon the congregation grows restless by looking at their watches. In this moment the speaker starts to anticipate the restlessness of the congregation and starts to announce that he is "closing" or "coming down" which ultimately cuts his intended message in half just to please the flesh. After he hurriedly tries to deliver his last few points, (because there is always something more to be said) the service is wrapped up with a closing song after which announcements are read and the benediction is recited. Next service, we will do the same thing and the routine continues. Unfortunately, a better job was done quenching the Holy Spirit than what was offered in the actual contents of the service. Were believers satisfied? Were their needs met?

Where was God in all of these rituals? Was He magnified or glorified? Did He receive the praise, worship, thanksgiving and adoration that He deserves? Was His name exalted? Is this all we have to offer such an awesome God for bringing us through the week? It seems so insufficient and inadequate for all His mercies. Yet the grace of God is so sufficient that we could never pay Him for what He has done and continues to do for us even though our praise and worship fails heavily in comparison to His enduring mercies. Do you believe that was enough time spent with the man who loves you unconditionally enough to suffer humiliation and give His life on your behalf? But, we get to see just how much we need Him because we could never repay Him for all His goodness towards us. In Psalms 116:12, the psalmist asked the question, "What shall I render unto the Lord for all his benefits toward me? We certainly are not worthy of Gods' benefits because of our good deeds or because of our righteousness. The prophet Isaiah likens our righteousness to that of filthy rags.[Isaiah 64:6] Even though we are undeserving of God's love, He still guides and protects us.

And to put things in perspective, what are we really running home from church to do anyhow? Watch the television? Gossip on the phone or go to the movies? How about spending time in the arms of an unmarried spouse? These are some of the reasons why believers and visitors sometimes leave church miserable and more burdened down than when they first came. Sometimes believers leave church feeling that they did not get anything out of the service or that the service was boring. These are all reasons stemming from a service where God was not present. In the presence of God there is fullness of joy and at His right hand, there are pleasures forevermore. Praise and worship is not a ritual to be manipulated or to see how long it should continue. Moreover it is not a competition to see who can sing the best or the loudest. Praise and worship is always about giving God recognition for who He is and what He has done. It is about extolling Him to the highest praise and exalting Him above everything and everyone else.

What happens when you praise God?

²¹ And when he had consulted with the people, he appointed singers unto the Lord, and that should praise the beauty of holiness, as they went out before the army, and to say, Praise the Lord; for his mercy endureth for ever.

²² And when they began to sing and to praise, the Lord set ambushments against the children of Ammon, Moab, and mount Seir, which were come against Judah; and they were smitten. ²Chronicles 20:21-22 (KJV)

It is a known phrase that "When the praises go up, the blessings come down." And although it is a common cliché used by many, unfortunately it is not written verbatim in the bible. But, true to its meaning, it simply re-enforces the fact that when you pay homage to God by praising Him with all your heart, then He will keep His promises and pour out His blessings. When you praise God, not just with your lips, but when you start to magnify, revere and worship Him in spirit and honesty; then deliverance, healing, and protection will be your portion as referenced above in 2 Chronicles chapter 20. Praising God will reap the believer blessings and favor in return. Praise is not only to sing a collection of fast songs to the genre of music that you like, neither is worship the singing of slow songs only. What is noise to you may be the height of praises to others. What sounds dead to you may be the depth of worship for someone else. Therefore, praise is personal. The next time you are in an environment where the people are shouting and dancing clamorously and the drums are pounding in a loud but joyful manner, do not criticize them, join in and give God some praise. This type of worship is a kind of *Hallal* and *Zamar* praise which will be explained later in the types of praise we can offer up to the Lord. The intensity of your praise determines the outcome of your breakthrough and victory.

How should we praise?

Praise and worship involves the entire body and anything that can make a sound.

> [3] Praise him with the sound of the trumpet: praise him with the psaltery and harp.
>
> [4] Praise him with the timbrel and dance: praise him with stringed instruments and organs.
>
> [5] Praise him upon the loud cymbals: praise him upon the high sounding cymbals.[Psalms 150:3-5 (KJV)]

David commanded his entire being to praise the Lord. In Psalms 103:1 he writes: Bless the Lord, O my soul: and all that is within me, bless his holy name.(KJV)

When we take a literal analysis to what David was trying to say, we see that he wanted not just his soul but his mind, his organs, his tissues, cells and literally his entire body to bless God. In the English language, there is no other word for praise, however, the Hebrew language names 7 different ways of proclaiming praises before God using members of our body in various postures and also with musical instruments *(The Complete Word Study Dictionary, Baker, Carpenter)*.

1. **Todah:** Thanksgiving, hands lifted with the palms turn up. Thanking God for all His benefits.
2. **Yadah:** Hands extended in worship with strength and confidence towards heaven. (Baker, Carpenter)

3. **Hallal:** To shine, boast over God, be clamorously foolish, to celebrate God, to dance and get out of yourself with joy. Similarly to David when he danced out of his clothes.
4. **Tehillah:** To sing spontaneously, glorifying God through singing in the spirit.
5. **Shabach:** To shout with a loud voice; get loud, to command and triumph.
6. **Barak:** To kneel down, bowing back and forward in adoration to God.
7. **Zamar:** The playing of instruments, singing, praising, and plucking the strings of musical instruments with joyful expression.

Without praise, we cannot pray effectively. We would only be praying from intellect reciting powerless words we already know. Sincere praise is imbued with power. And when power penetrates our prayers, praise becomes easier which then takes us into another realm of worship. "Enter into his gates with thanksgiving and into his courts with praise." What does this mean?

The Old Testament references very specific ways God required praise. Any arbitrary unclean vessel could not offer up praise as it would not be accepted and the offender risked death if certain traditions were not followed. The Moses tabernacle was a place set apart to meet God to worship. It is an oblong court, fenced all around with fine white linen, copper and silver poles, and a blue, red, purple and white hand woven embroidered material. The tabernacle had three sections: The outer court, the Holy place (inner court) and the Holies of Holies. To the rear end of the Tabernacle sits the Tent which consists of the Holy Place and the Holies of Holies. Covering the tent is the four-layered woven embroidery to protect the furniture on the inside. To enter the tabernacle, the worshipper must enter into what is called the outer court through a gate. In this section were a brazen altar and the brazen laver (a basin like container) on a stand with a mirror and water inside. The brazen altar was where the priest offered up daily animal sacrifices on behalf of the people for their sins. He would then wash in the brazen laver as a sign of cleansing and purification before he was qualified to enter the Holy place (inner court) to send up praises. In the inner court, grace and mercy was obtained through praise and prayer. God's dwelling place was in the Holies of Holies where His power and anointing flowed. It is here that the Ark of the Covenant was seated which contained the Torah (Law of God), Aaron's rod and a jar of manna. Only the High priest with a chain tied around his waist could enter this sacred place once per year to intercede for the people; if he were not pure, he would not come out alive; hence, he would be pulled out by the chain.

This Old Testament example serves as a reminder and an indication that we should set apart and dedicate a special place in our home where we meet and spend quality time with God. Even though the method to reach God has changed, His principles and process to seek Him has not. The praises to God should be purposed and already be in the heart and flowing out of the mouth of every believer. Thanksgiving began even before the worshipper reached the outer court. Remember he says "enter into His gates with thanksgiving and into His courts with praise." In other words, as born again saints we should already have praises in our heart before we get to church. When we strive to get in the presence of God from home and stay in the spirit of worship, we can then take notice of the difference in our praise and worship during the service. It becomes much easier and joyful as opposed to a dreaded ritual.

You may sometimes wonder why your prayers feel like they are bouncing back from the roof or why you cannot seem to get a breakthrough in the spiritual realm. This is because your mind has become a playground for the enemy to do his tricks and cause you to be become distracted. To get a breakthrough in prayer, praise or worship we must first cleanse ourselves, an emptying and an outpouring before God. This happens when you give yourself away, when flesh dies, when your mind, body and soul are all on one accord. Remember the scriptures say that those who worship must worship in spirit and in truth.

My fellow believers; praise and worship should not be limited to being inside a church building but praise can be rendered from home, on the job and even while driving. It is Satan's intention to destroy you with every opportunity; on the highway through an accident, at home through your family, on the job through co-workers and supervisors and even in the church through members and leaders. So, it is imperative that our worship be of substance to counteract the wiles of the devil.

Praise, worship, prayer and fasting go hand in hand: they each play a unique role in the effectiveness of service. The flesh does not readily want to praise God so we must train our inner man by seeking the Lord continuously through prayer and fasting so that it is dominant during worship. Also, it is my strong recommendation to praise and worship leaders to make sure to invite the presence of God into your service by first praying the prayer of repentance before engaging the congregation in thanksgiving and adoration. Choose songs that have meaning relevant to life's situation, needs and circumstances. Do not rush a song to get to the other. Linger on one song if you must until a revelation of what is being sung penetrates the congregation. Feel the presence of God ushering in the anointing in the sanctuary so that the spirit of God can lead. This is also the time when worship becomes personal; your voice should decrease while the Holy Ghost starts ministering to individual needs resulting in a collective spiritual fire, reminiscent of the days of Pentecost. The same applies to the congregation as well even if not a part of the praise and worship team. Stay in the presence of God until the spirit of heaviness disappears.

When we praise God we are praising Him for what he has already done, what He is doing and what He is about to do. The next time you are praising God, be sure to listen keenly to your words. Anyone or anything that can make a sound, or make noise rather can offer praise; but it takes a sold out, dedicated, God-fearing individual to worship. Worshiping in spirit and in truth means to free your mind from all cares of life and meet God at the throne of worship. The heart of a true worshiper will still embrace God through the pain, through the hurt, through the pending foreclosure on the home, or even when the car is repossessed. A sincere worshiper will still exalt God even after the loss of a job, when there is no food, and when the children are rebelling. If you can still make the time to meet God, love on Him like never before and tell Him how much you adore and need Him despite the pain and suffering then that is authentic worship. Expect Him to show up and show off on your behalf. He will not leave His children forsaken and He is working it out through your worship. The faint in heart cannot worship God. There is a difference between one who worships and one who praises. One can praise without worship but you cannot worship without praise; it is impossible. Believers, I dare you to start worshiping and see what will happen.

Take a close look at this Tabernacle, can you picture yourself there? from the outer court to the inner court, getting ready to to meet God in His Holy and secret Place. Just you and Him. Take a praise and worship break and give God what is due to Him.

Image: Goodseed International, 2000

Prayer & Praise Page

Omnipotent God of Moses you are worthy to be praised. How majestic is your name oh God and how magnificent are your attributes. I give you glory, honor and praise. Father you are awesome and superb and I long to bask in your embrace. Omniscient father you know everything and I surrender to you my master and my king. Lord, I know we were born to worship you therefore I lay my sins before you; those that I've willfully committed and those that I've unknowingly omitted. Father I am sorry for neglecting sincere praise and worship but I thank you for extending to me the garment of praise that replaces the spirit of heaviness. Sweet Jesus, as of today I command my mouth, my hands, my feet, my spirit and my entire body to praise you. Forgive my prideful and self-centered attitude and teach me how to worship you in spirit and in truth. Lord, show me how to get self out of the way and how to enter fully in your presence. Teach me how to worship in spite of my circumstances and regardless of my surroundings. Father your word says let everything that have breath praise you, so with every breath in me, I shout Hallelujah! Hallelujah! Glory to God! Thank you Jesus! Thank you Lord for loving me and for looking beyond my faults and seeing my needs! Glory Hallelujah; blessed is the name of the most-high God. Jehovah Jireh, thank you for being my provider. Jehovah Nissi, thank you for wrapping your arms around me. Jehovah Shammah, thank you for always being there, Jehovah Rophe, thank you for your healing power. Glory to your matchless name! Hallelujah! Holy Ghost I want to get beyond mere praise and into the arena of worship where the enemy cannot distract me causing me to think on the cares of life and become agitated. Father, fill me with your power and fresh anointing of worship in Jesus precious name. Hallelujah!

God is a Spirit: and they that worship him must worship him in spirit and in truth. John 4:24

Chapter 10

Whom Do You Feed First?

*P*hilippians 3:19 Whose end is destruction, whose God is their belly, and whose glory is in their shame, who mind earthly things.

Food is a necessary part of life. Without food we can only live for a period of time. Food provides the body with essential vitamins, minerals and nourishment and from it we gain strength, energy and fuel to carry out our daily functions. If a certain nutrient is missing from our diet, or worse, if we consume too much of one thing, it will show in our appearance and subsequently affect our health, whether it be good or bad. The spiritual man operates in much the same fashion. If we do not feed our spiritual man, he becomes weak, powerless and inefficient.

Have you ever notice that as soon as you walk into your house, the first thing you do is head straight to the refrigerator or to the stove, lifting pot covers to see if there is food. Why does this happen all the time? The mind is constantly reminding the body that it needs food to sustain its vital organs. Most of the time however, the body is not hungry; sometimes dehydration can trigger our hunger reflex and send us scrambling into the kitchen. Water and liquids is a necessary component to keep us from dehydration. Much the same way, the spiritual man needs fuel to function. If we do not live in God's word and commit ourselves to prayer and fasting, food for the spirit, then our spiritual man will become weak, starved and unequipped to stave off temptation and keep us in a realm of praise.

The following is an example of how the mind can trick the body into thinking it wants or needs food. Have you ever been on the road travelling and as soon as you see someone eating, you want that same thing that they are having? Or as soon as you get a glimpse of Wendy's, McDonald's or Burger King you suddenly have to stop and get something. You may only have the last five dollars in your pocket but your mind convinced you that your craving was worth satisfying.

Now think about a time when you were busy taking care of business for the entire day and could scarcely think about food. It seems as if you could have passed a million food chains but did not stop because you were either too busy or had no money. Did your mind intervene then? No, because you were consciously aware that you had no money. Were you hungry? Did your body need food? Yes of course but did you die? No, you waited until you reached home. Sometimes our need for food is really driven by the mind or the lust of what the eye sees. Our mind works against us similarly to how the enemy plots against us to detour our thoughts from doing the will of God.

Let us review the scenario again: On the day that you were not hungry but had money, you stopped to satisfy your fast food craving because you saw someone eating something you like or drove by one of your favorite fast food chains. Adversely, on the day you had no money, you were hungry but you were not tempted or drawn into a food place. This is exactly what the enemy does to us. He entices and tricks us and we fall for his temptations over and over again; then he laughs and leaves us on our own to suffer the consequences.

The same way we constantly seek to feed our flesh should be the same way in which we diligently seek food for our spiritual man. We feed our natural bodies every day so why do we have a tendency to wait until Sunday or Saturday, depending on the day we worship, to satisfy our spiritual man? The physical body suffers great side effects when being fed the wrong foods. Likewise, the spiritual man suffers when it is absorbed with the wrong things. When the physical man flourishes because of nutrients in your diet so will the spiritual man flourish and prosper when it is being fed on time, all the time and with the right type of food.

> Beloved, I wish above all things that thou mayest prosper
> and be in health, even as thy soul prospereth. 3 John 1:2 (KJV)

Foods that nourish the spiritual man are prayer. Not gossiping and backbiting: Reading the bible, not watching soap operas or horror movies; Praise and worship, not seeking fame and fortune. Too many times we miss the mark because we stop pressing. We lose our first love for Jesus Christ. The fire that once ignited our passion to seek God and the things of God is gone. The fire on the altar is out and your light is hidden under a bushel. Therefore, the spirit becomes restless because he is starving. God wants us to be an example to the world; guidance for the ignorant, a leader for followers and a teacher for the novice. He wants us to help win souls to populate heaven. We cannot be equipped to do so if we constantly starve our spirit.

God does not want us to be of the world trying to see how we can get to the top. He is not concerned with whom is within our social networks or with which dignitary we have met. God wants to use us to promote His glory not what we can do of ourselves. There is nothing wrong with having ambitions or earthly goals but it should not become our sole focus so that we become neglectful of the spiritual man. These are some of the reasons why the spiritual man malfunction and deteriorate because we love and value material things instead of loving the things of God. We should aim to attain the characteristics and attributes of God. Timothy warns us that the love of money is the root of all evil which comes with dire consequences and serious affliction.

1 Timothy 6:10-12

> [10] For the love of money is the root of all evil: which while some coveted after, they have erred from the faith, and pierced themselves through with many sorrows.

> [11] But thou, O man of God, flee these things; and follow after righteousness, godliness, faith, love, patience, meekness.

[12] Fight the good fight of faith, lay hold on eternal life, whereunto thou art also called, and hast professed a good profession before many witnesses. King James Version (KJV)

By that same token, God is not interested, impressed, or moved by what we used to do in the past. I hear many Christians brag about what they "used to do" for the Lord and how they once were on fire in the church. They rave and ramble about how they used to pray all night; sing on the choir, lay hands on the sick and prophesy with results. My encouragement to my "used to" believers is to start feeding the spiritual man again and turn that "used to" attitude into action. God is interested in our future, impressed by our diligence and moved by our willingness to act now.

Do you realize that when you "used to" do all these things that it was because your spiritual man was being fed? You spent more time with God reading the Bible praying and fasting and gaining from the Lord. How can we get back to our first love for God? Well, it takes work. Unfortunately, it is much easier to pick up a spoon or fork and start to feed our natural bodies than it is to feed our spiritual man through fasting and praying. It is actually a little more challenging because it does not come as second nature to us and therefore we have to will our stubborn flesh to go against what it is naturally accustomed to having or doing. One of the first things I recommend in getting back to this place is to do a spiritual fast. Fasting not only cleanses the mind, body and soul but it sets us up to be in a place where we can hear from God. The next section addresses some of the ways believers can fast and see results. Often, we pray and continue to pray without seeing the results of our prayers and this is because the scriptures firmly mentions that some things do not get remedied without the combination of fasting and prayer. Matthew 17:21 says "Howbeit this kind goeth not out but by prayer and fasting." (KJV)

Prayer Page

Mighty God of Zion, with a convicted conscience and tears flowing down my face I humbly seek your help, mercy and forgiveness. Father I am in a state of brokenness and I know you will not despise my broken spirit nor my contrite heart. God, I cry out to you this evening because I am guilty of excessively feeding my flesh and allowing my inner man to undergo spiritual famine which results in my spiritual malnutrition. God, I know it's your perfect will for me to be in good health.

Father I am overcome by the temptation of the flesh. I answer every call it makes for food and rebelliously ignore my spiritual man screaming for help because it is starving. Master; forgive me, forgive me, Oh Lord I am sincerely pleading for mercy. Father let not my physical man suffer the consequences it deserves because of my immature behavior.

Lord, I rebuke, I renounce, I denounce and bind up the onset of stroke, heart attack, diabetes, embolisms, asthma, atherosclerosis, ulcers, cancer, hypertension, edema, migraine or any other health condition that can result from my gluttony or overfeeding the flesh. Hear my cry o Lord; give a listening ear to my call. Daddy Jesus you have sent your word to heal. The words from this chapter are like a double-edged sword that cuts me on the way in and on the way out. I am convicted to the core and my eyes are open to see the inevitable. God I am so sorry. God I need your help to restrain the flesh. Without you I'm a complete failure. Thank you Jesus for loving me enough to show me the deadly path on which I am traveling. Thank you Lord.

. . . It is written, Man shall not live by bread alone, but by every word that proceedeth out of the mouth of God. Matt 4:4

Chapter 11

Fasting: Do's & Don'ts
Is it still relevant?

Matthew 6:16-18

> [16] Moreover **when ye fast**, be not, as the hypocrites, of a sad countenance: for they disfigure their faces, that they may appear unto men to fast. Verily I say unto you, They have their reward.

> [17] But thou, **when thou fastest**, anoint thine head, and wash thy face;

> [18] That thou appear not unto men to fast, but unto thy Father which is in secret: and thy Father, which seeth in secret, shall reward thee openly. (KJV)

I have found from experience that fasting is one of the best investments a believer can make. It has unlimited benefits when done correctly. Fasting supercharges your spiritual life, takes you to the next level with Christ and empowers you for the task ahead. Many Christians today believe that fasting is useless and has no value. The opposite, however, is true. It is sometimes practiced in vain by some because of misunderstandings as to its real purpose. Fasting is not an easy endeavor: it is a challenging undertaking because the flesh does not want to be deprived from food. Sadly, whenever it is time to fast, that is the time when it seems as if the body is starved and wants to eat every second. Yet, on a regular day, you will go all day without food unaware. Why? Because Satan knows prayer and fasting release power and spells trouble for his domain. Therefore, he tries to sabotage your every effort to fast.

Even the secular world realizes the value of fasting and has benefited from it tremendously. I am reminded of a true story written by Dave Williams about two elderly men, one 70 years of age and the other in his eighties. The 70 year old suffered from multiple health issues including asthma, which was the worst of all. His doctor told him to go on an extended supervised fast. After six days his enlarged prostate went back to the size of a young man and his sinuses cleared. His breathing was back to normal and on the 36th day, a miracle took place: He regained hearing in his deaf ear. A few days later, astonishingly, he was no longer impotent. Even though doctors know fasting is beneficial for our health, I am sure neither he nor the patient expected all these drastic changes at once.

The man in his eighties is Dave's grandfather. He was diagnosed with cancer and was told he had to have surgery or else he would only live for a few months. He insisted he would not do the surgery but instead went home and changed his diet. From his farm, he got all fruits, vegetables, and rhubarb and ate them for breakfast, lunch and dinner. Dave stated that not only did he live out the rest of the year but he lived another 16 years and when he died, it was not from cancer. Fasting enhances one's health by detoxing and eliminating waste matter from the body. Studies show that fasting removes dying and diseased cells. And even though fasting has superb health benefits, it was not the primary reason for fasting in the olden days nor should it be the only reason we fast today. Fasting has many spiritual benefits including God's intervention in unbearable and impossible situations.

What is fasting?

Fasting means to sacrifice. It is a conscious turning away from the plate and voluntarily abstaining from consuming food or liquid for a certain period of time or days while seeking God's direction and intervention. According to John R. Rice, "Fasting, then, should mean that one determines to seek the face of God and for a time, at least, to abstain from other things in order to give the whole heart to prayer and waiting on God. Fasting and prayer means to leave off the lesser blessings for the greater one, the lesser duty for the far more important duty." Fasting is also a way to humble oneself before God therefore it involves sacrificially putting away pleasant and satisfying things: watching television, abstaining from visiting social networks or even attending some of your favorite places. It is a designated time away from everything comfortable and to focus on Christ. There are so many things in our daily lives that distract us from the word of God and compete for our attention. Therefore, fasting requires an active effort so that we do not rob ourselves of much needed time with the Lord. During fasting, the flesh has to conform to the spirit because it is subdued with the combination of prayer. Fasting disciplines the flesh and the spirit which brings us to total dependency on God.

When you are fasting, you should try at all costs to eliminate distractions. Try to avoid telephone conversations that are not edifying or events that do not feed you spiritually. If possible, it is probably best not to engage in extended phone conversations during your fast and especially right before you expect to break your fast. The same discipline is required if you are in the midst of praying, reading the bible or worshiping. As believers, we must be very alert when fasting because the devil awaits us for opportunities where he can inflict the most damage. Do you remember when God asked Satan, "From whence comest thou?" The devil answered, "From going to and fro the earth and from walking up and down in it." (Job 2:2). Peter warns to be sober, vigilant; because your adversary the devil, as a roaring lion, walketh about, seeking whom he may devour. (1 Peter 5:8.) Satan will make sure he alerts someone to call you on the phone with some disturbing news to stop your breakthrough, disrupt your peace and cause you to be irritable and eventually get you out of the presence of God, causing your fasting to become futile. Not engaging in phone conversation or turning off the television is using wisdom so as to not become distracted.

There are various kinds of fasting mentioned in the bible. The most popular fasts practiced today are:

Absolute Fast: No food or water

Examples: Moses, Esther, Ezra, Paul, King of Nineveh

Moses

Exodus 34:27-28

> [27] And the Lord said unto Moses, Write thou these words: for after the tenor of these words I have made a covenant with thee and with Israel.

> [28] And he was there with the Lord forty days and forty nights; he did neither eat bread, nor drink water. And he wrote upon the tables the words of the covenant, the ten commandments. King James Version (KJV)

Esther

Esther 4:16

> [16] Go, gather together all the Jews that are present in Shushan, and fast ye for me, and neither eat nor drink three days, night or day: I also and my maidens will fast likewise; and so will I go in unto the king, which is not according to the law: and if I perish, I perish. King James Version (KJV)

Ezra

Ezra 10:6

⁶ Then Ezra rose up from before the house of God, and went into the chamber of Johanan the son of Eliashib: and when he came thither, he did eat no bread, nor drink water: for he mourned because of the transgression of them that had been carried away. King James Version (KJV)

Paul

Acts 9:8-9

⁸ And Saul arose from the earth; and when his eyes were opened, he saw no man: but they led him by the hand, and brought him into Damascus.

⁹ And he was three days without sight, and neither did eat nor drink. King James Version (KJV)

Nineveh

Jonah 3:5-10

⁵ So the people of Nineveh believed God, and proclaimed a fast, and put on sackcloth, from the greatest of them even to the least of them.

⁶ For word came unto the king of Nineveh, and he arose from his throne, and he laid his robe from him, and covered him with sackcloth, and sat in ashes.

⁷ And he caused it to be proclaimed and published through Nineveh by the decree of the king and his nobles, saying, Let neither man nor beast, herd nor flock, taste any thing: let them not feed, nor drink water:

⁸ But let man and beast be covered with sackcloth, and cry mightily unto God: yea, let them turn every one from his evil way, and from the violence that is in their hands.

⁹ Who can tell if God will turn and repent, and turn away from his fierce anger, that we perish not?

¹⁰ And God saw their works, that they turned from their evil way; and God repented of the evil, that he had said that he would do unto them; and he did it not. King James Version (KJV)

Normal Fast: No food but water only

Examples: Jesus Christ

Jesus Christ

Matthew 4:1-2

4 Then was Jesus led up of the Spirit into the wilderness to be tempted of the devil.

² And when he had fasted forty days and forty nights, he was afterward an hungred. King James Version (KJV)

Partial Fast: Specific foods and liquids
(e.g. vegetables, grains, fruits, salads, water, natural vegetable or fruit juice. Daniel 1:11-15 and Daniel 10:2-3)

Example: Daniel

Daniel 10:2-3
> [2] In those days I Daniel was mourning three full weeks.
>
> [3] I ate no pleasant bread, neither came flesh nor wine in my mouth, neither did I anoint myself at all, till three whole weeks were fulfilled. King James Version (KJV)

Why should we fast?

According to Pastor Steven Holt, author of *"The Power of Fasting and Prayer,"* there are certain problems so deep and powerful in a person, city, or nation, that the problem cannot be solved outside of great fasting and prayer. It would seem that the fasting and prayer of Mordecai and then the Jews (Esther 4-10) were the means by which God turned tragedy into triumph against the evil forces working in and through Haman.

Fasting varies according to each individual's need and situation. People fast for many different reasons. There are those who fast to build a relationship with God and get closer to Him. Some people fast to seek and receive God's wisdom concerning spiritual warfare, making life changing decisions or to purge sin from their lives. There are also those who fast for clarity and direction when choosing a mate, a business partner, or a leader for the ministry. Additionally, one should fast when feeling oppressed or burdened by spirits of heaviness. Fasting is the ideal weapon to cancel Satan's plot over our lives and those of our families and friends. Fasting for revelation about direction for the future is also not a bad idea. Isaiah 58 tells us we should fast to break the bonds of witchcraft, to undo heavy burden, to feed, clothe and shelter the poor, and to free the oppressed. Remember, it is always a great idea to fast before making any drastic life changing decisions.

Fasting not only defeat the mission of the enemy but puts us on guard and shield us from attacks from principalities and forces in high places.

> "It would seem from the passage in Ephesians 6:12 that just as there are hierarchies of angels available to do the work of God, there are also corresponding hierarchies of demonic powers that constantly work to sabotage and destroy God's work. In the case of Daniel, the answer from God could not reach him without 21 days of fasting and prayer! The means by which the answer came was through a higher, more powerful angel binding the demon over Persia and thus releasing God's power to Daniel.
>
> Again we see this principle at work as Jesus dealt with a demonically influenced boy of whom the disciples tried unsuccessfully to release from an evil spirit. After Jesus had freed the young man from the evil spirit, he explained to his inquisitive disciples the reason why they were unable to free the boy. Jesus said, "This kind (kind of demon) cannot come out by anything but prayer and fasting." (Mark 9:29) Prayer with fasting is needed to breakthrough spiritual forces that hinder or block God's answer to our prayers. Thus, it is no wonder that every great revival has been preceded by great seasons of prayer and, with certain men, coupled with fasting." (Steven Holt, *The Power of Fasting and Prayer*)

Old Testament references in support of fasting:

A. <u>**Fasting in times of conflict (War):**</u>

* The Israelites fasted at Bethel in the battle against the children of Benjamin. (Judges 20:26)
* The Israelites fasted at Mizpeh during the war with the Philistines. (1 Samuel 7:6)

B. <u>**Fasting for the sick or deceased:**</u>

* David fasted for his sick son.
* Fasting seven days for Saul's death. (1Chronicles 10:12, 1Samuel 31:13)
* Jonathan's death (2 Samuel 1:2)

C. <u>**Fasting for God's forgiveness:**</u>

* Moses fasted 40 days because of Israel's sin. (Deuteronomy 9:15-18)
* Ahab fasted to be forgiven (1Kings21:17-29)
* Nineveh fasted at the preaching of Jonah (Jonah 3:4-10)
* Ezra did a general fast (Nehemiah 9:1-3)
* Daniel fasted as he confessed the sin of Israel (Daniel 9:3-5)
* Joel call the people to return to him in fasting, rending their hearts and not their garment. (Joel 2:12-15)

D. <u>**Fasting in times of Pending danger**</u>:

* Mordecai fasted due to the decree that was to be carried out by Haman (Esther 4:3)

E. <u>**Fasting to commemorate certain events:**</u>

* The Israelites fasted in commemoration. (Jeremiah 52:12-13)

New Testament references in support of fasting

* Jesus fasted in the wilderness (Matthew 4:2 & Luke 4:2)
* Jesus says this kind of demon cannot be cast out except through fasting and prayer (Matthew 17:21)
* Jesus disciples, "then shall they fast in those days" after the bridegroom is taken from them. (Luke 5:35)
* Paul and Barnabas fast and prayed seeking God's direction to appoint elders for the church. (Acts 14:23)
* When Saul was on his way to Damascus he encountered Jesus, and then his name, intentions and attitude were changed after he fasted three days. (Acts 9:9)
* While Cornelius was fasting and praying an angel appeared to him with instruction to call for Peter. (Acts 10:30)
* In addition to Paul's physical hardship, pain and affliction, he finds time to feed his soul through fasting. (2 Corinthians 6:5, 11:27)

How should you fast?

It is my recommendation that during fasting, it is ideal to make yourself a prayer list. Include names of people for whom you would like to pray and the reasons for which you will be fasting. Next to each item, also make a notation of the revelation that will be imparted to you by the Lord. Be certain to spend time reading the word and to pray as often as possible. Praying is sometimes the best way to ward off the pangs of hunger. For your morning regimen, begin by praying through your prayer list. At mid-day you can change your position by offering praises unto the Lord followed by prayer, reading the word and worship. The same goes for the evening but additionally, you can take the time to meditate on God's goodness and His mercy. In addition to the bible, it is also a good idea to equip yourself with motivational and inspirational material to keep your mind occupied throughout the day (for example, books, audio tapes, gospel compact discs, etc.)

Be certain that the motive for your fasting lines up with the word and the will of God. Fasting should be a time of enthusiasm as you will be praying to open the heart of God. Fast with expectancy!

When should you fast?

Fasting is a mighty weapon that destroys Satan's plan, sends confusion in his camp, frustrates his agents and moves God on our side. As such, we should strive to fast as often as possible. We live in a world where Satan and his comrades are in dominion and as a result, we are in constant persecution from the enemy. It really does not matter which hour one chooses to fast as long as it is done in sincerity. Most people choose sunrise to sunset 6a.m. to 6p.m. Some choose 6 a.m. to noon or even extend it to 2 p.m. to fit into their work schedule. There are times you may be prompted to do a one day absolute fast (24hrs no eating or drinking). Depending on the nature of your needs you may choose to do 3 days, 7 days, 10 days, 21 days or even 40 days. A Pastor once told me that he does not fast at all unless he has a serious problem and that he does not get up and fast arbitrarily like he sees others do. In his ignorance he proclaimed, "That is not how fasting works." In response I said, there is so much going on in and around us yet alone what is seen and heard on the news and in the newspaper. I remembered thinking, no wonder he only had five members and what seemed to be a lifeless church. Audaciously enough, he asked me what can he do to get people in his church and if I would come and work with him.

Believers, it is my sole conviction that fasting is a necessity. It is an effective spiritual tool especially in the aforementioned example where it was obvious to me this pastor had a prideful oppressive spirit which was causing his church to be complacent. His church would definitely be in a better position if he were to call for a unified fast among his brethren. Again, fasting and prayer can reap a multitude of benefits.

Pastors and leaders please do not wait for the first week of January to call a corporate fast for your church. It seems to be an empty ritual in most churches today. Members, likewise, do not wait for someone to tell you to fast. Fasting can be an individual effort and is very effective. Satan and his comrades are an organized union; they too go on regular fasting to get things done. While you are waiting and relaxing, they are working. Fasting comes with short-term pain but a long-term gain.

What to avoid during a fast

Fasting is a sacrificial offering unto God. It is a time where you seek direction, clarity and guidance from the Lord. It is also a time of humbling oneself before the Lord. As such, it is best to avoid distractions in all forms. While you are abstaining from food, you should also try and abstain from secular ungodly things that will cause you to lose focus. Yes this includes abstaining from your favorite television programs and social media outlets. Avoid too much chatter on the telephone, which sometimes open the door for gossiping. This is also a time to feed your soul and edify your inner man so any other reading material except the bible is not recommended. Avoid music that is not uplifting to the soul and if possible avoid contact with people such as friends or family whom you know will cause you to lose sight and get involved in unwanted activities.

There are individuals who think there is nothing to do while on fasting so they sleep all day. This too is unacceptable. Fasting places the flesh in discomfort and the spiritual man in power. So any excessive sleeping that diminishes the time the flesh is in peril is prohibited. There are also times when believers are on fasting and get so involved and caught up with what is happening in their environment they forget they are on a fast. At all cost, try to avoid seeking attention or any arguments that may lead to strife.

During fasting it is very dangerous not to be alert and aware. Whenever you are fasting, your spirit is now open and susceptible to good as well as evil. And unfortunately, it is evil that usually takes pre-eminence in readily presenting itself if we are not careful. Have you ever notice that when fasting for answers on a particular matter, the situation got worse instead before it got better? This is a result of neglecting to guard the spirit. The enemy uses this opportunity to leave you more wounded than before you started fasting.

Can you fast while at work? Absolutely: but with wisdom. While fasting in the presence of others, it is best to be discrete and talk less. Remember fasting is unto the Lord and should not be heralded to your neighbors. Jesus warned against behaviors like these when he reprimanded the Sadducees for doing their alms before men and disfigured their faces as an indication to their peers that they fasted. The Sadducees sought the praises of man. It is always best to fast in solitude with limited activity even though it is not always possible. Stay away from social or common areas like the lunchroom where you might become tempted to eat or join in the gossip which will contaminate your ear passages and your spirit. Be serious about your fast so it will not turn out to be a hunger strike in which God takes no pleasure. Isaiah 58:3.

My personal way to fast

I like to initiate fasting with the prayer of repentance. In it I pray for guidance and for the Lord to guard my mind and spirit. I specifically ask the Lord for wisdom as sometimes we fast but do not know the areas of our lives for which a fast is needed. I ask for knowledge to understand the scriptures I will be reading and in addition, I pray that all interference from distracting spirits will be restrained and rendered powerless. I then commit myself to reading the bible. I do not rush through the scriptures; I pause and meditate on what I read then seek clarity and revelation. It is so exciting to seek answers from the Lord and to see how diligent He is in responding. After this regimen, I uplift myself with some gospel music followed by prayer, praise and worship. I often listen to and reflect on sermons from someone else and then I start singing. I normally continue like this until it is time to break the fast. When I keep it flowing like this, my mind is constantly occupied with the things of God while the atmosphere around me is saturated with His presence. This way Satan has no loophole to push through. I am in perfect peace because my mind is continuously stayed on God. My days and times may vary but I prefer to fast from 6 p.m. to midnight or to 6a.m. Most importantly, I make sure to stay diligent for the duration of the fast.

What happens during and after a fast?

Fasting restrains demons, pull down strong-holds and move us in the direction that the Lord intended. It brings joy and success and grants protection in our lives.

When believers begin to fast, Satan moves in for the kill. He distracts us in every way possible so as to throw us off our intended course. Maybe the children start misbehaving in the worst rebellious way or your spouse finds everything to create an argument. On the job, wickedness starts to brew and in the church the spirit of strife raises its head. Sometimes, unexpectedly, you may develop a health condition or find yourself in a financial plight. Nevertheless, if you stand your grounds and yield not to temptation you will overcome. It is only a test for you to lose your blessing. Remind yourself that whatever hurtful words or deeds are thrown at you, it is not about you but what is on the inside of you. Moreover, they are being used as a tool from the hand of Satan.

After a careful review of all the scriptures on fasting, with Jesus serving as the ultimate example saying not "if" we fast but "when" we fast, I am convinced that fasting is relevant today. It is imperative for born-again believers to engage themselves and practice fasting with the right motive on a regular basis. A great change awaits your prayer life, physical life and spiritual life. In spite of the struggles, the reward is great. Fear not! There is still power in prayer.

M, McGriff (personal communication) July 2011

Prayer

Dear God my master and my king, you reign mighty over the universe and my entire being. You are my strength when I am weak; you are my refuge in the time of trouble. Father I approach your throne of mercy in request for the will power to make fasting a part of my Christian walk. Lord, I want to be empowered, I want to be anointed and most importantly, I want to have a closer relationship with you. Lord I really didn't think fasting was that important to our spiritual growth, now I have read and understand that you not only set the example by fasting but left instructions for us on how to keep fasting. Lord, the fact that you said your disciples will need to fast when you are gone has opened my eyes even more to the need for fasting in my own life.

Holy Spirit, I know food is a necessity for my earthly body and without your help, fasting will be a challenge. I am asking your help to curb my fleshly appetite and instead fill me with a yearning to know more of your goodness. I ask for direction and the will power to be victorious over the flesh and yield not to temptation in Jesus name. Amen.

Beloved, I wish above all things that thou mayest prosper and be in health, even as thy soul prospereth. 3John1:2

Chapter 12

Spiritual Warfare: What you need to know

Spiritual warfare: What is that?

I am by no means attempting to write or teach on spiritual warfare as it is a very wide and intense subject. I just want to give a glimpse of what it entails, **what entertains** it and **how to fight**, **win and stay victorious**. Spiritual warfare is synonymous to physical war but you cannot see with your naked eyes what or with whom you are fighting. It is an on-going battle between the forces; good and evil, light and darkness. There are demonic spirits, human spirits and Satan himself who wages war against us minutely through our mind, action, feelings, will, co-workers, family and church family. Even unbelievers encounter spiritual warfare which they sometime can't identify so they call it bad luck, misfortune, coincidence, or they blame the people around them. Most sickness and disease, generational curses, repetitive mishaps in one's life or relationships is a form of spiritual warfare. Insanity, depression, instability and confusion of the mind are just a few; the list is endless. For example, if you are working twenty four hours a day for most of your life and still have no savings, assets or emergency funds, this is a spiritual war on your finances. If you can identify something that is ongoing in your life that only occurs a certain time of the year or month, chances are it is because of spiritual warfare.

Many times individuals are unaware of the things in their homes or surroundings that leave an open door and have become a magnet to principalities and powers which results in the **entertainmen**t of evil spirits. Ouija boards used to connect one to the dark world, talisman, charms, crystal stones and balls, candles and incense burning, figurines and some paintings are some of the things that have demonic powers attached to them. Again, the list is endless. Unfortunately, the churches today are ignorant to spiritual warfare. They do not have a clue what it is, how to engage it, or how to win it and stay victorious. Furthermore, they take everything lightly and at face value and pay no attention to what is happening in and around their lives. I prefer to engage in warfare prayers if a strand of my hair hurts and later find out that it was not warfare, than not to engage at all and then be defeated. Even the preacher who gets on the pulpit and preaches nothing else but material gain and milking the congregation for their last dime is undergoing a spiritual warfare in the flesh unaware.

They are being attack by the spirit of mammon. What is that? Mammon is a spirit that governs money. They are driven by the need for money and more money. In addition, it hinders them from preaching and teaching the unadulterated word of the living God. This is why believers are still being oppressed, depressed, possessed, and bound and naïve about spiritual warfare. They do not preach or teach how to live right outside of the church neither the importance of repentance and salvation. Romans 10:14 says how shall they hear without a preacher? God's people are destroyed because of what they do not know and refuse to learn. There are many weapons to fight spiritual wars but believers must know what they are and how to use them. What good is a soldiers' weapon if he hasn't the slightest clue how to use them? To name a few: praying in tongues confounds the enemy because he does not understand it. Moreover, this is the Holy Spirit making intercession for us because we do not know how to pray. Praise and worship is another weapon that gets the attention of God and move Him to dispatch His angels on our behalf. Prayer and fasting, and the written word of God binds, loose, tear down, strengthen and protects. In order to get the victory and stay victorious you must keep yourself in the presence of God. Stay dressed in your spiritual bulletproof vest. And most importantly, keep your heart clean and pure.

Dear Reader,

One could scarcely write a book on the effectiveness of prayer without giving some examples of how prayer has changed his or her life or the lives of others around them.

This next section addresses real life accounts of testimonies from personal or individual experiences. The testimonies are relayed from a first-hand perspective to preserve the impact of the message.

God works in and through his people so that they become instruments declaring His handy work. All praises and honor belongs to the almighty father as His name is glorified in the heavens and the earth.

Love,
Jasmine

Chapter 13

Individual Testimonials

Testimony: 9 Days to Live

Recently, I mean as recent as Sunday May 27, 2012 the Lord showed me in a vision a woman sitting on a bench. She was lifeless and in pain. She was groaning and moaning and her groaning grew louder by the minute. In the vision, the Lord said, "Jas go get a bottle of olive oil and pour it on the woman's head but do not touch her. You don't have much time; Hurry! They gave her 9 days to live which ends tomorrow (Monday) at 12 o'clock." I awoke from the vision at 6:15 a.m. While I was laying there worried and pondering whom this woman might be, I heard the voice again saying, "You need to get up and pray; you don't have much time, get up! Go! As a matter of fact, I want you to go on fasting, put nothing in your mouth before 6 p.m."

Still nervous, I went to work not knowing who the woman was or if the woman in the dream could have been me. Upon reaching work, the voice came again saying, "Someone's life is on the line; go pray." I began searching the scriptures and continued reading the bible and afterwards went into prayer and that is when it was revealed to me whom was given the 9 days to live. I was not aware of her being sick or facing any challenges at that time. Frightening as it seemed I sent the woman a text message saying, "Woman of God it is well; I am fasting for you." I did not disclose the reason. She responded that she was supposed to be in the hospital from Friday but had told the Lord that He has to come through for her because she did not want to go to the hospital.

When I realized the extent of the warfare, I immediately called for re-enforcement from my prayer partners in Jamaica instructing them to start applying the blood of Jesus at 5 minutes before noon or exactly at noon. I also gave the same instruction to the woman who had 9 days to live. Throughout the day, I would send her words or scriptures of encouragement as the Lord gave it to me. The fast ended at 6 p.m. as directed by God but she did not know when the fast ended. Approximately 6:45p.m. I received a text message from her saying, "Sister Jasmine I am asking you please continue to stay close and live for the Lord; continue to be obedient to His voice. I am feeling much better now and was able to go outside for the first time since Friday. I could not even go to the living room. Thanks and God bless you."

I was lead to go on three days fasting on her behalf. She eventually went to the hospital three days later where she was diagnosed with some lung condition according to the doctor. She was hospitalized for a period of time, most of which she spent in the Intensive Care Unit but was then later sent home with oxygen which did nothing to help her condition. I was privileged to see and spend a little time with her on July 6 while I was visiting Jamaica. She could hardly catch her breath to speak but she stated that was one of her better days. Nonetheless, we were able to exchange thoughts. She proceeded to share a few encounters and experiences with me and she was very sharp and alert. What she saw and felt were the exact things that were being done to her in the spiritual realm. After listening to her, I broke the news that she was the one given 9 days to live. "I thought as much," she replied. Hey, the vision was in May, it is now July and even though she is still a bit under the weather, she is still alive all glory to God.

Sadly, on Monday the 30th day of July, she lost the strength to fight for her body but won the war for her soul. When the news came that she died my first question was whether or not she had passed away during the midday hour. Her daughter informed me yes. Immediately I knew the enemy had gone and renewed the assignment that was broken before through the power of prayer and fasting. Remember that eight weeks prior she was given 9 days to live which should have ended on a Monday at noon according to the vision I had and had only shared with a few people shortly after I saw it. Who was this woman? She was a 37 year old Pastor and one of my dear friends. How can a mighty woman of God die at the hand of witchcraft?

First, we must realize that the spiritual world is actively real and powerful. Be reminded of the scripture, "Fear not the one that kill the body but fear the one that can kill both body and soul." Which means it is possible for something or someone to kill you. Remember the story of Stephen in the Old Testament and countless others. Do not forget Simon the sorcerer, the witch of Endor, and Pharaoh with all his magicians who tried to imitate God's power by activating their evil powers. This is to serve as a reminder that we have been and is still in a real battle. Witchcraft is real and respects no one. Furthermore, it is one of Satan's tactic used against human beings. As fictional as it may seem, I am saddened to announce that it is quite common for leaders, pastors and other believers to die at the hand of witchcraft. My first pastor in N.Y. died from a witchcraft attack in 2008. Once again, the doctors said it was a lung condition. This is the reason why we cannot be ignorant to the devils vices or underestimate him or his agents. We are no match for the devil. Nevertheless, all things work together for good to them that love the Lord. Regardless of what it may be, at the end of the day, God will get the glory through that tragedy. She is a wounded soldier but she won the war.

Think of an undisputed, undefeated heavy weight boxer in the ring. Because his opponent knows the champions' potential, the opponent will repeatedly pound him on the lower body muscles. His intention is to wear him out so he can become weak and slow down. As a result, there is a strong possibility for a knock out followed by a defeat. The same is true for a powerful child of God when he or she is beaten physically or spiritually and all strength is gone. Defeat is inevitable especially if there is no one to war or travail on his or her behalf. I felt guilty for my friend's death because I rested and quit fighting for her after the victory. I should have continued in intercessory prayer until she was totally out of the woods. For that, I partially took some of the blame and pointed a finger towards the church who knew of her illness but only prayed what I call a weak ice-cream prayer and refused to continue fighting on her behalf. Through prayer and fasting, the death assignment for her life was cancelled. But because the enemy sought her relentlessly, he was able to prosper when her veil of protection was weakened. As believers, we celebrate and rest after a victory and quit after a defeat. On the other hand, Satan regroups after a defeat, strategizes how he can better get the job done and try again. When he gains a victory, he says yes! One down a few more to go and continues; even if he has to rotate workers to accomplish his goal. Believe it, Satan is that organized. Her death is an untimely premature death and could have been prevented. The bible says he reveals to redeem.

Fear not! There is still power in prayer.

Testimony: Boy Never Talked Nor Walked

A few years ago, a dear friend of mine by the name of Evangelist Vendrix Headley and I went to a church to minister. During the service, a certain woman brought a baby to another woman that was sitting next to me for approximately five minutes. The baby looked to be anywhere from nine to eleven months old. His eyes and limbs were so weak and his frail body seemed lifeless. Immediately I started crying and fighting with something on the inside of me that I could not explain. I felt so sorry for the baby even though I did not know him. I thought to myself maybe the short space of time he came next to me was an informal introduction letting me know that my assignment was to pray for him. But I quickly dismiss that thought. Church was about to dismiss when the visiting Pastor called a few of us on the pulpit to sing. As soon as I stepped on the pulpit, my eyes browsed over the congregation but my focus came back to where the woman and the baby were sitting. I no longer resist so I called her to come forward and took the child from her.

As soon as I took the child, I noticed he was getting heavier and heavier by the minute. A thought came to mind to give him back to his mother but then another thought said to hold the child, so I kept holding him. Instantly I observed his features started to change. Now it was noticeable that his entire eyes were looking directly at me. Then with a pleasant look on his face, his little hands started reaching towards my face. He became so lively and kept reaching out to play with my face so I allowed him. I started talking to him in a baby-like voice and telling him to say Hallelujah and he did. I repeated it a few times and he repeated it as a baby would. Then the church started rejoicing and worshiping. I did not give much attention to the actions of the baby nor the response of the congregation because I thought the baby's actions were normal.

While he was still in my hand, it was impressed upon me to let him stand so I allowed him to stand, holding his hand as I started to lead him in the same mannerisms normally taken when teaching a baby to walk. He took three steps and the members who saw went into a frenzy of praise. Again, ok, they are excited to see the baby starting to walk, I whispered. Wow! A very large woman ran from the other side of the church picks up the baby, put him across her broad back as if she is putting on a belt and started to stretch him. The child was crying hysterically then she took him from off her back and started beating the bottom of his feet. She started to explain that she too had a son who would not walk and this is what she did for him to start walking. Would you believe that the baby did not take another step that day? If only I knew at the time what I know now.

Later, I found out that the child who I thought was a baby was actually 5 years old. He has never uttered a word or ever walked before and that was the reason why the church got so excited when he said Hallelujah and took those steps. I was shown another little boy, healthy and vibrant, running around the church having fun and they said that was his twin brother. I was privileged to speak with his mother who told me he was diagnosed with meningitis a few months after he was born "He is now twelve years old; unfortunately he is still not walking or talking but he is very smart," she said. I knew for certain that God was about to work a gigantic miracle him that day and the enemy stepped in and interfered through the spirit of divination. His deliverance was blocked that day but it cannot be stopped.

It is very important for believers to have the spirit of discernment to see beyond a pretty face and discern thoughts and motives. Discernment makes us aware of good and evil. Because I was a young Christian, I did not know or understand much and I thought everyone that claimed the name of Jesus, prophesy few words that are true and speak in tongues are real born again Christian. I am reminded of Paul in the book of Acts during his evangelism services where a young woman following him saying this is surely a man of God. Even though what she was saying was true, Paul rebuked her because she was operating under the spirit of divination. Nevertheless, fear not! There is still power in prayer.

Testimony: Barred by Immigration

There was a young woman who came to the United States undocumented but was privileged to attend school and then went on to college. To protect her identity, I will refer to her as Sandy. She got married to a United States army soldier who was later called over to Germany before being deployed to Iraq. Because they just got married and was expecting their first child, he decided he would not leave her behind. They then went together to the United States Immigration to obtain the necessary documentation which would enable her to leave and return to the United States without any problem. She was given a package containing the requested documents for the German Immigration. She was reassured that everything was well so with confidence she and her husband left for Germany.

Because Sandy was told by the United States Immigration that she had up to three years to gather her documentation with the German Immigration, she waited until after the birth of her child. Approximately a year and a half later after being in Germany, she decided to go to the immigration office. Upon arriving there, she handed them the package from the United States only to find out that she would not be granted re-entry because she broke the law by residing there illegally. Sandy was told she has to go back to her land of birth for ten years then re-apply for a re-entry to the United States.

Sandy called her mom who was in the U.S. to inform her of the dilemma. Her mom was devastated by the news and the thought of her only daughter going back to a place she does not know and have no knowledge. And, she was worried about not being able to see her daughter for ten years. I remember my sister calling to tell me about the situation and ask me to call Sandy's mother so she could explain to me what had happened. I called Sandy's mother with some encouraging words and reassured her that her daughter would not be sent back to her country and that she will be back in the United States. She was very pessimistic but I kept on reminding her about the undefeated power of God and the things He is doing behind the scenes on our behalf and that we have no clue of how He is working it out but He is, if only we could get a glimpse.

Nonetheless, mom gathered enough strength to call every prayer group and praying individual known to her requesting prayer for her daughter's freedom and divine intervention from God. Sandy's mother prayed night and day twenty four hours around the clock. She even made mention of a unique experience she encountered while in prayer with a prayer group called "Silent Unity." Her words were, "while the individual was praying, I felt so light, it's as if I was levitating with an outer body experience. I have never experience such divine connection before." And the next morning on her way to work, she opened her mouth to start praying for her daughter when she heard a voice said, "Don't pray for Sandy anymore."

In addition to all the prayers, the pivotal point came to a head when Sandy's mother-in-law went to Washington and gave them a peace of her mind. One can assume what she must have said but her sentiments were clear. After her son had laid down his life without reservation for this country, depriving his first born of a daddy, his wife from a husband and ripped his only comfort from his heart, this is no way to pay him back and say thanks. Approximately two weeks later, Sandy got a letter in the mail from the German Immigration. She did not fully understand the contents but was fearful to go and find out. Nevertheless, she became bold and went a few weeks later to inquire about the meaning of the letter. The officer asked, "You are still here? You have 36 hours to leave

Germany." One afternoon while I was at work, I received a call from Sandy's mother saying, "Sandy is home in the United States of America and I just want to say thanks to all the people who prayed."

Even with all of the prayers and petitions, it does not negate the fact that Sandy broke the law. But in hindsight, let him that is without sin cast the first stone is the thought that came to mind. Jesus did not come to condemn but to call people who break the law to repentance. May I remind you of Proverbs 21:1 that says, "The king's heart is in the hand of the Lord, as the rivers of water: He turneth it whithersoever He will." When men say no, God says yes! When man closes doors, God opens them. When man say it's over, He says it just began. God specializes in things that seem impossible. His perfect will must be done on Earth as it is in Heaven and it was written in Heaven that it was not His will for Sandy to go back to her country. Not only was she sent back to America from Germany but she was later granted her green card and is now a citizen. All power has to be subjected to the higher powers of God.

Fear not! There is still power in prayer.

Testimony: Unable to Belch

One morning in June of 2011, I received a phone call. Upon answering the phone I heard an unfamiliar male voice on the other end saying, "Hi Jasmine, how are you?" "I am blessed and highly favored, who wants to know?" I responded. "Sam from the Cayman Island," He replied. A friend who allowed me to listen to your gospel and prayer CD's gave me your number and I am interested in getting a few more of your CD's he stated. After we had been conversing for a while, I realized he was an old associate.

During our conversation, I sensed that there were spiritual warfare surrounding him and was trying my best not to be involved but the Holy Ghost would have it the other way around. Sam later asked me to pray with him. After praying, I asked him about a bottle of water that I saw in the spirit. "My hand is on it right now as we speak," he replied. "Ok let me prayer over the water," I replied. "You need to go on a 3-day fast and drink that water!" I told Sam. The next day he called back, "Jasmine one of the weirdest things happened last night after I ate my dinner. I was just belching non-stop." "That's not weird it's probably gas" I responded. "You don't understand I have not belched in 2 years," he explained. A few days later, Sam called again. We talked for a while about the goodness of God then he mentioned the reduction of his belly. "What do you mean?" I asked. "I went on the 3-day fast and drank the water, after which I noticed my belly went down; it was so big" he says. Thank God, I am feeling much better now.

Later on, I asked the mutual friend who gave Sam the CD if indeed it was true that Sam had a big belly which was no longer there. My friend chuckled and said yes Sam had looked like he was 9 months pregnant. Not that I doubted Sam but I really thought he was exaggerating.

Fear not there is still power in prayer!

Testimony: Lesbians on the Train

One winter evening in New York, I stood at the train station eagerly waiting for the train to arrive. Hey, it's New York so it is known that the stations can get pretty crowded. Amidst the crowded platform were two outstanding young ladies presumably in their late teens, kissing and fondling each other in a sexual manner. One of them was a little more daring than the other and I was a bit annoyed. I held the newspaper in front of my face just to ignore what was happening. "Oh, thank you Jesus the train is here," I exclaimed as I hurried unto the train with a sense of relief that I would be travelling in a direction opposite where they were going. Was I wrong! Not only did they come in the same car of the train as I but was also sitting directly across from me still kissing and fondling each other. I decided enough was enough and there was no way I was going to tolerate this anymore. Of course I was not going to create a scene so I did everything underneath my breath.

I started praying, "In the name of Jesus I rebuke and bind up every lesbian spirit on this train." "Satan I command you through the power in the blood of Jesus Christ to take your filthy hands off the lives of these young ladies; loose them and set them free from these fowl spirit. And I cast them out into outer darkness in Jesus mighty name." Demons can hear you no matter how softly you speak.

Reader, not even two minutes passed after that prayer was uttered when the young lady who was a little laid back started having an attitude with the daring partner. She started cursing and yelling, "Leave me alone, don't touch me; are you deaf? What's wrong with you? Stop! Take your hands off me." Little miss daring was so frightened she froze with her mouth wide open steering at her. Then the daring partner finally said, "What's up with you? What got into you all of a sudden?" Remember, they were sitting directly in front of me so I could hear every word. Shortly after, little miss daring reached her destination. Her partner angrily yelled to her again saying "Go home! Go wash yourself." Little miss daring hissed her teeth and got off the train. Do not underestimate the power of prayer.

Fear Not! There is still power in prayer.

Testimony: Gays on the Train: Part 2 (About 40 minutes later)

While still in transit on another train from Manhattan to Queens, I encountered the same disgusting behavior on display only that this time, it was between two men. I immediately speak to the situation with boldness and authority I did not pray a long prayer. I said, God! Again, no more that is enough let your will be done in the lives of these two men.

Immediately, there was a visible change, the young man who was enjoying being touched all of a sudden did not want his friend to touch him anymore. Each time his partner put his hand on his leg he would remove it with disgust. Between his teeth and under his breath he was whispering, "Stop!" With fear on his face, he kept looking around to see if anyone was watching. Don't forget the Lord has given you power over all the powers of the enemy. Whatever situation you face or may face, the power lies in your mouth to defeat it from the root. God is no respecter of persons. Call on Him In challenging situation. God does not wear hearing aids and He is certainly not deaf.

Fear not there is still power in prayer!

Testimony: Dunamis Power to the DMV

One night in New York on my way home from church, I was pulled over twice by the police. The first time, I had three of my church sisters with me and the officer did not ask for any documents nor did he give any warning. Upon approaching the car, he just told me to go. On the second stop I wasn't so lucky. The officer approached my window and asked for my documents. I pulled my seat belt to retrieve them from the glove compartment and as I handed them to him he said, "Ma'am you were not wearing your seat belt." "Sir, you saw when I pull my belt to get you the papers," I responded. He handed me a ticket for not wearing my seat belt and said if I don't like it then I can see him in court. At the time, my driver's license was suspended and I was doing over time on what is call a conditional license. A conditional license is a license given to you by the DMV, upon application if your regular driver's license is suspended. It permits you to drive for certain amount of hours within a day for approximately six months if my memory serves me correctly. I don't understand why their system did not show the suspension when he pulled me over but thanks be to almighty God.

Nevertheless, I decided to take my chances and go to court. There was a piece of document needed for the court that I could only obtain through the Division of Motor Vehicles (DMV) which would also show the status of my driver's license. Ouch! Upon arriving at the DMV counter I requested the document for the court. The receptionist printed two copies. Afterwards I noticed a frown on her face as she printed them again. When the new copies came out, she looked at them, looked at me and then called the attention of one of her colleagues. Now both of them started looking at me weird.

"Who are you?" she asked as she began printing for the third time. This time she seemed a bit confused, hissed her teeth and just stood there amazed. I asked her if there was a problem, "yes, and I do not understand this, who are you?" she continued. "One of the documents is showing your license is suspended and the other is showing it has been reinstated." "Which one is for the judge?" I asked. "The piece that says reinstated and the one that says suspended is for you" she replied. "Can I have them?" I asked. "Even if I explained, you would not understand" I continued. She then hurriedly gave them to me and with her hands in the air she said to me "Go!" I went to the court, sat there nervous but patiently waiting for my name to be called. The court's officer started the roll call but my name was nowhere on the list so he asked my name and my reason for being there. I handed him the ticket; he gave it to the judge and to my surprise, the police officer who gave me the ticket was not in court. The judge looked at me and said, "Miss Gordon, your case is dismissed." The ticket was thrown out. In tears, I lifted my hands in the courtroom and shouted "Thank you Jesus!" I went home praising God.

When your ways please God, he will allow favor to defend you! I am swimming in the ocean of favor.

Testimony: Dunamis Power to the DMV, Part 2: (Months later in Virginia)

My son wanted to attend school in Virginia where my sister lives but I needed to show proof of residence in order to get him enrolled. One Friday evening, my sister accompanied me and we went to the Division of Motor Vehicles (DMV) to change over my driver's license. The wait was exceptionally long but when my number was called I went to the counter, stood there for a while and waited for them to process my documents. Shortly thereafter the clerk said, "Ma'am our system just went down and I am not sure how long it will be before it comes back and we are about to close for the day. Come back on Monday."

Monday came but my sister was unable to accompany me so she asked one of her friends to take me. Her friend took me to another DMV closer to her home. I went to the counter and in the process of retrieving my driving records; she said oops, our system just went down. "How long will it be?" I asked. With a smile she responded, "I am not sure, are you jinxing us? "What do you mean? What is jinxing?" I enquired. "I see where you went to the other DMV on Friday and were unable to get it done because their system went down" she explained. "It's alright, go back there and get your picture taken in the mean while" she said. Twenty minutes later the system was back up and running. Even though I had a conditional license from New York as my name was called, I became nervous thinking that they would deny me because of the suspension on my regular license. Once again, the favor of God shined on me without my input. The receptionist handed me my new driver's license. This is what happens when you put the ALMIGHTY God first. You will walk with His power and His glory will surround you like an armor. He will overturn any verdict, cancel any suspensions and move any mountain or hindrance on your behalf. Pray without ceasing.

Fear not there is still power in prayer.

Testimony: The Toe Starts To Grow

There is a woman in Jamaica who had two of her toes removed because of diabetes. While in Jamaica, I went to visit her daughter Trish and she was there. "Can you anoint my feet and pray for me?" she asked. While I anointed her feet I asked her if she thinks her toes would grow back. "Oh no!" she responded. "The doctor removed them and they won't grow back" she stated. I insisted they could grow back; however, we left it there. I went back to Jamaica the following year and gave her daughter a bottle of olive oil to give to her. I jokingly said to Trish "tell your mom don't be surprised if her toes grow back." I sent the message to tease her because she said they wouldn't. I know nothing is impossible for God to do even though it has been and still is my prayer to see creative miracles in my ministry.

Months later her daughter called with utmost excitement. "Jasmine, guess what? Mommy's toe is growing back." I said ok and asked if she is sure and how does she know. "I saw it myself; I saw the little nail pushing forward" she responded. I revisited Jamaica again in 2011 and on our way home we stopped by the woman's house. Of course, I was curious to see the toe. Upon arrival, I inquired "May I see your toe that Trish said is growing back?"

To my surprise, there is indeed a little nail that started to push forward. Be reminded, your words have power. It is written, life and death lies in the power of your tongue and according to St. Mark 11:23 you shall have what you say.

Fear not there is still power in prayer!

Testimony: Sibling Rivalry for 2 Years

My sister is my best friend; my counselor, my mentor, my go to person, my twin really albeit a six year age difference. She is my blood sister born from the same mother and father. But, something went radically wrong between us in fall of 2000. At the time, neither of us was born again and there was just something about my persona that she could not stand. During that time, we had a perfect phone relationship but as soon as she entered my house, her mood changes. Until this day, I cannot tell what the real cause of our rivalry was. Things got from bad to worse and what used to be an inseparable relationship, was now totally sour. So sour that I invited her to our mother's 74th birthday party, the first birthday party in my mother's life and my sister did not show up. On many occasions, I tried reaching out to her leaving her favorite gifts at her house but she would not give me the time of day.

In the summer of 2002, I was born again and I invited her to my baptism but she did not come. In 2003, I invited her to my graduation from the "Manhattan Bible Institute" and again she did not come, neither did she return any of my calls. Now I started feeling very disappointed. Nevertheless, I was saved now and learning to take everything to God in prayer. In March of the same year, I started praying radically for the restoration of a better relationship between my sister and I. I started rooting up the spirit of anger, bitterness, un-forgiveness, hate and malice and replaced them with love, joy, peace, forgiveness and compassion. I prayed for her to have restless days and sleepless nights until she acknowledged and accepted Jesus Christ as Lord and Savior. I no longer tried to reach her I just kept on praying and left it in the care of the omnipotent one.

In May of the same year, exactly two months later I went home from work one evening, played my answering machine and heard a very familiar voice but could not figure it out right away. I played it over and over again just to be sure I was hearing correctly. The message said, "I don't know why I am calling you but um, I, I, um, I don't know why I am calling you but I guess we need to talk, um please give me a call." It was my sister! "Yes!" I shouted and started praising God. I did not return her call that evening. The next day I went to work, wanted to call her but wasn't sure what the mood would be like, what to say or even where to begin. I knew if I continued to ponder, I would keep on delaying so I got bold and made the call. Surprisingly, there was no tension between us. We reminisce on the past, discussed the present and made plans for the future.

During our conversation, she mentioned again that she didn't know why she called but she was restless. I started laughing. "That has been my prayers for you to be restless and have sleepless nights until you accept Jesus Christ," I told her. "Ha-ha, so you are the reason why I can't sleep at nights," she responded. We spoke for approximately two hours but who knows; maybe if we weren't at work we would have continued the conversation as we both have the gift of gab. Today our relationship exceeds what it used to be and I am proud to announce that my sister is born again. She is now a prayer warrior, an intercessor, and a powerful woman of God. She has grown to be a woman hungry for the knowledge of God and a woman who is now helping to mend relationships and lending a listening ear to others. There is no situation or relationship too far-gone that God cannot renew or turn around. The heart of man is in God's hand and He can turn it wherever He will. He is waiting on your prayer.

Fear not there is still power in prayer!

Testimony: Hitting Rock Bottom

Just before I was saved in 2002 I hit rock bottom. My license for work was expired and neither the state nor the facilities in which I worked wanted to renew it because of the length of time it was expired. Shortly after that, my driver's license was suspended and I could not use my car because it too was suspended which left me with no income. I had rent to pay, a child going to school and little to no food. For those who do not know that vehicles can be suspended; when a car is suspended, it means no one else can register or insure it even if they have a valid driver's license. With no choice, I started working as a security officer. With so little income, I was unable to meet my demands. I shared my situation with an associate, who encouraged me to start making extra income from buying and selling goods. I immediately objected as my pride insisted that having to resort to buying and selling is far beneath me. Additionally, I did not want to risk being seen by friends and co-workers who knew what prestigious positions I used to hold.

My income was not getting any better so I had to swallow my pride and turn to buying and selling. I was robbed a few times but I thank God it was not life threatening. As I recall, on the 4th of July, I was getting ready to leave the house for my place of business when I was approached by my son who was 16 years old at the time. With tears in his eyes, he begged me not to go out that day. I explained to him all the reasons why I had to go. He looked at me, now fully crying, and said "Mommy, please don't go, it's the 4th of July and its crazy out there, anything can happen." "Don't go mommy, God will provide." I started crying and decided to stay home. Looking at his innocent face and hearing his persuasive voice I just couldn't disobey. Perhaps it was the Lord speaking through him.

The location where I sold goods was approximately one mile from home and many nights I walked home at 2 or 3 a.m. dragging my little red bag behind me crying and talking to God. I was asking him why I was going through all of this. I said, "God I want to be saved." "Lord why can't I be saved? Did I blaspheme?" "What did I do wrong?" I was so frustrated, confused and restless. On this particular evening while at my place of business, a couple stopped by. They started witnessing and encouraging me to give my life to God. They invited me to church and promised they would come and pick me up from home. As they were about to leave, the husband reached in his pocket and gave me fifteen dollars. I thought he wanted to make a purchase but he said "no, that's yours." Oh no, now I felt lower than dirt. I know he did it from his heart but I started crying and wondering if I looked that deprived and needy.

Pride aside, I took the fifteen dollars and bought a dress for church. Sunday morning came and the couple arrived early to take me to church as they promised. All this began in June 2002. I then started going to church on a regular basis until I finally surrendered my heart to Jesus Christ. In August of that same year, I woke up one morning and felt sick and tired of living beneath my Godly privileges. I decided that I was going on fasting for seven days. Often, I remembered seeing the results of my mother's fast. I decided I would make fasting part of my regular routine. I would get up in the morning still in my night clothes, hair not combed but I was reading my bible and praying from 6a.m. to 6p.m. I was saved but I was not yet baptized. Reflecting back, I remember that as a young babe in Christ I was eager to fast and looked forward to it even though I did not know if I was doing it correctly.

On the seventh day of the fast, my phone rang. It was an agency that I was trying to get into for over 2 years prior but to no avail. They called me with a job offer that would require me to work for six days. I gladly took it. After a week on that job, another agency called with an irresistible offer. Now what do I do? I worked with both agencies for awhile until I gave up one of them. In the same month of August my license for work was renewed and my car and driver's license was restored. I was happy serving my God. I was later baptized in December 2002.

Sometimes God has to allow us to go down a rough pathway so we can look up to Him. When we are broken, only He can mend us the way we ought to be. When restless, we can find comfort in Him. And when deserted, we are left to seek Him. Readers if you are going through your valley experience, don't give up, don't quit and don't throw in the towel. You may be knocked down but not knocked out. Remember it's in the valley that he restores; it's from the valley He exalts, and it's in the valley you will gain strength. Do not look on the depth of the valley or how rough the side of the mountain. The depth of the valley signifies that you are being set apart for greater use later and the roughness of the mountain enables you to flex your spiritual muscles. When God is getting ready to do greatness in your life, things seem to get worse. He came through for me and without a doubt; He will do the same for you. Hold on and be encouraged and fear not as there is still power in prayer.

Special thanks to Brother Alvin Walters and Sister "P" who is now Pastor Portia Owen Walters. Keep on winning souls for the kingdom of God. I am one of your fruit, exhibiting the greatness of God.

Testimony: The Eleventh hour

In February 2012, I was sent to a cancer patient's home to be his nurse for the night. Upon arrival, all his family members were present. He was restless and uncomfortable from the excruciating pain rocking his body but he was alert enough to hold a constructive conversation. On top of his agony, he bled profusely from his rectum. I asked his daughter if he had gotten a blood transfusion. She replied yes but the doctor said it would only last for six months. That day had marked the sixth month. Finally, the opportunity came where it was only he and I in the room. I started a conversation with him about the Lord and he was receptive. I asked him if he was saved or if he had a church home. "No" was his reply. I told him that I would like to introduce him to a man by the name of Jesus who forgive sins, heal the sick and take away pain and I asked if he would you like to meet him. He responded "Yes." Then I asked him to pray the prayer of repentance after me and he did.

Friends, immediately after he prayed the prayer he lay still on the bed. He was no longer twisting and turning. I asked if he was feeling any better and he responded, "Yea a little better; the pain is not so intense" he said. I then prayed for him and he fell asleep. Eight hours later, he died. I was stunned and left with many questions. What were the odds that I was present at this man's house to minister and lead him to Christ eight hours before he died? Was that written in God's plan when I was born forty-one years ago thousands of miles away? Perhaps I was asking what seemed to be dumb questions. But even though we know that nothing is too hard or impossible for God, sometimes we face some experiences that make us wonder and this was one of those situations.

In the same year in June 2012, my own brother on the island of Jamaica was hospitalized with cancer. I wanted to visit him after Father's day because I had other commitments. But the Lord said to me I did not have that much time and with the encouragement of a friend, I went to see my brother the weekend before Father's day. Upon arrival, I sat at his bedside holding his hand, briefly ministering to him about God as he was not saved. I said to him, "Your physical house, your body, has deteriorated and it is now time for you to be relocated." "In your current condition you can no longer work for the Lord but He is neither resentful nor revengeful." "In fact, God does not want your body He wants your soul" I made it clear to my brother that, whether he believes or receives the Lord as his Lord and savior, He (God) still loves him. I advised him not to look through the rear view mirror on that which he had left behind but to look through the windshield and see what lies ahead. I continued ministering to him, "I have nothing else to give you other than Jesus, are you willing and ready to say yes to Him?" I asked, "Yes", he responded. I lead him to pray the prayer of repentance and when he was done, he tightly squeezed my hand. "Thank you my sister," he said. Then in tears, he cried out, "God help me!"

I returned to the States where the following Saturday morning I had the opportunity to reinforce the love of Jesus over the phone to my brother. I reminded him that he is now saved and reassured him that he is in good hands so therefore it is alright to let go and let God. My brother was unable to speak due to his condition but I said to him "Even though I know you are not able to answer me, I want you to know we all love you and in your mind, I want you to say, Jesus my heart is yours, my mind is yours, my will is yours." He responded with a few muffled sounds. Then his daughter took the phone and said, "Aunty now you are making me cry!" "Why" I asked. "Because daddy is crying," she replied.

I thought to myself, a broken spirit and a contrite heart the Lord will not despise. Nearly three hours later, a text came in stating, "He is gone." My brother passed away the day before father's day. Thank God, I obeyed and went to visit in the time that I had. Each time I think about the events that transpired before his death, I rejoice and am comforted by the story of the thief on the cross who was saved at the eleventh hour. I never shed a tear until now that I am writing about him. Beloved, this is how much God loves us: He will make certain that everyone has the opportunity to hear of His love and salvation so that the individual can make their choice. It is not God's will for any of us to be separated from Him. God is fair and He gives us all the opportunity to choose eternal life. Whom or what will you choose? Are you sure you will get the same opportunity as my patient and my brother? Do you know if you have enough time?

Testimony: Fibroid Disappears after 28 years: Delrose's Story

As a young girl, I was troubled with severe abdominal pains. It happened often but was especially noticeable during my monthly cycle. The pain was so unbearable that I had to see a doctor, whom after a thorough check, told me there is a small fibroid growing inside me. Although the fibroid was as small as a lime, she mentioned that it can pose a problem should I become pregnant.

In 2006, I remember visiting a church in Bronx New York. After morning service dismissed, the Pastor of the church came over to introduce himself and then asked if I was saved or if I had accepted Jesus Christ as my Lord and savior. I remember his encouraging words which remain with me even to this day.

After the midday session, I went to his office to speak with him on a different matter and the subject of health entered our conversation. It was a perfect segue for me to mention that I was diagnosed with fibroids which had now grown to the size of a grapefruit. I remember telling him that surgery was not an option I wanted, his response was that surgery is one of the many ways that God heals. I reluctantly agreed with him but strongly advised that I did not want to undergo surgery as I am depending on God to heal me. I did not know when or how long it was going to take but I knew God was more than capable and so I was going to believe and wait on Him for a miracle. Moreover, I was afraid to do surgery. So I left it at the altar where I prayed and believed God to show up on behalf of my circumstances. Without a shadow of doubt, I wanted God to heal me and believed that I would be healed without surgery. I kept speaking my healing into existence and would not back down.

Years went by and nothing happened; it seemed as if the fibroid was getting bigger and causing more issues. Over the years, I kept requesting prayer from individuals and from various prayer lines but I never gave up. In January of 2009, during an early Monday morning prayer meeting that the church held regularly, the question was asked if there was anyone in the midst with fibroids. I raised my hand and was then called to the altar where the saints prayed for me. I returned to my seat in the congregation but the fibroid was still there. I went home and kept feeling my stomach but it was still there. The fibroid felt so hard, it was as if I was pregnant. Many times I would go and lay on my back just to feel and see if it was gone but it was still there. I grew very anxious because I was expecting God to heal me so I anticipated every moment by continually checking to see when it would leave.

Monday after Monday I kept going back to the early morning prayer with the saints. It was a time of worship and celebration and praise to God. When I reached the church, I would normally stay towards the back of the building so I could mind God's business by worshiping and adoring Him in prayer and praise. During this service however, one of the church sisters came to anoint me with some olive oil. She did not ask if the fibroid was gone she instead asked me to raise my blouse so she could anoint my stomach all the way reaching towards my back. And without saying a word she returned to the front of the church where she sat.

After the prayer meeting I went to work. I kept feeling on my stomach but the fibroid was still there. After work, I went home and again felt my stomach but it was still there. With a sigh, I kept on feeling my stomach as I know prayer works so why was the fibroid still there? A few days later, I was at work when I felt the warmth of a trickle running down my legs. The trickle erupted in a big gush which sent me rushing to the bathroom. To my surprise I had excreted what could have easily been clots but I did not know what they were at the time as I had never seen anything like this before. I thought it was just the fibroid getting worse and causing me to lose so much blood. Truthfully, I use to fear having my cycle each month because I would be in excruciating pain. Worse, and much to my embarrassment; my menstruation flowed like a river and sometimes left a trail of mess wherever I sat.

As usual, I returned home from work and began my regular routine of checking my abdomen to see if I could still feel the hardened fibroid. I could not help but exclaim "Oh my God! My belly is soft! I squeezed and squeezed and pushed and pushed but did not feel the hardness any more. Wow! I said to myself. It is gone! It is gone! Thank you God!

Even though I had been experiencing the softness in my stomach for several months, I would still lay on my back daily to feel and see if it was true that the fibroid was gone. It was almost as if I could not believe it was true. After years and years; 28 years to be exact, of excruciating pain and suffering, I was finally healed. Today, I have no more pain and no more overflow at that time of the month. I am now comfortable in my body after 28 years of suffering.

Months later, I went to my gynecologist for my regular exam. I did not hear her mention anything about the fibroid so out of curiosity I asked her if the fibroid was still there. She immediately said no and asked what happened. I told her that God healed me. I did not have to do the surgery because God operated on me Himself. It is now three years later since my miracle took place and I am still fibroid free. All honor, glory and praise goes to almighty God, "Jehovah Raphe" the God that heals. Yes friends, he is still in the healing business.

My miracle took place in 2009. I am very happy to share my testimony and my personal experience of healing and deliverance through the power of prayer. This way, you too can be encouraged and know that there is hope once you believe.

Your suffering may be long but do not stop believing that God can and will heal you if it is His perfect will for your life. I say this because there are times when one dies and is never physically healed from their affliction; not that God is incapable, but He knows all things best. Moreover, sometimes our affliction keep us humble and in a better relationship with God. Be reminded of Paul's thorn in his flesh. He asked God three times to remove it and God answered that "His grace is sufficient; for [His] strength is made perfect in weakness."[2 Corinthians 12:8-9] Having said this, it is not for us to stop praying because God does change His mind depending on the persistency of the prayer. Although Hezekiah received notice that he would soon die, God heard his prayer and granted Him another fifteen years of life.

It is my opinion that when an individual's healing is not physically obvious; it is a possibility that God wants them to be humble. Think about it, we pray and seek God more when we have some form of ailment or trouble. Am I right? Keep on believing and expecting your healing and deliverance. He did it for Delrose and He can do it for you. It is evident that she questioned God but she never stopped believing that He would be faithful to His promise. He said by His stripes we are healed. Whatever we ask of Him; we will receive; so hold God to His words.

Fear not, there is still power in prayer!

Testimony: Barren For 17 years

On a beautiful sunny afternoon in December, I was on my way to work but decided to stroll around down town Montego Bay and window shop until it was time for work. While walking I ran into a friend, a sister in Christ. Our conversation varied. At one point, I stated to her that I was not feeling well but that I had an appointment to see the doctor. I did not share with her any details of the severity of the problem. We then started on the topic of prayer and then a discussion on God. I asked her if she has ever felt empty and dry; to the point where she cannot pray and even when she does if she feels as if it is going nowhere. She responded yes she has been there but that she knew a friend who is never tired of praying. She insisted on putting the friend's number in my phone so that I could contact her whenever I had the chance. She consoled me that her friend would pray for me and my problem.

Upon reaching work, I was contemplating whether or not I should call at that time or wait for later. I soon found boldness, however, and decided to call this stranger. She answered the phone and I introduced myself and told her how I got her number. We spoke briefly, because at that time, she was visiting Georgia and in the middle of fasting. She said she was not able to pray with me at the moment but that she would pray for me when she got the chance. On second thoughts, she then told me to call her later on that evening, but in the mean time ministered a few words of encouragement to me. I did not make mention of the excruciating pain I was feeling at the time but I heard her saying, "I rebuke that pain and cramp you are feeling in your belly right now in Jesus name". I was stunned because I know I did not tell my friend earlier and neither did I make mention of it to this woman.

I hung up the phone in amazement and of course, with questions. I asked, Lord, how did she know I was having issues with my belly and I did not mention it? Who is she? Then I quickly got a hold of myself and gave all glory to God knowing that nothing can be hidden from Him and that He is able to do exceedingly beyond what our little finite mind can comprehend. I realize that we are His eyes, hands and feet here on Earth and it is not His will for any of us to be beaten and defeated by Satan. Once we stay in His presence and seek Him wholeheartedly, He will reveal secrets and infirmities afflicting His children then send deliverance through His servants.

I could not wait to get home from work so I called my husband and told him what happened. He in turn asked the same question, "Who is this woman?" I told him that I did not know her personally and that she lives in the United States but that my friend told me she prays for people so I should call her. Now my curiosity was rising and anxiety starting to mount. I was anxious for night to fall because she told me to call her back in the evening and she would be able to pray with me then. That long awaited moment came and I called her. It seemed as if she had the phone in her hand waiting for me because she picked up immediately upon the first ring. She told me that after I hung up the phone earlier in the day she was lead to pray for me and for my family. While she was praying, she saw a teenage girl, perhaps my daughter or my niece, climbing out of a pit struggling to get free. The description of the clothes and the person she gave matched my daughter. I was stunned again because that same day while in down town Montego Bay, I was literally crying and asking God to deliver and save that specific daughter. She was more than a hand full to manage. I was so worried about this daughter that I would often have sleepless nights. However, the woman began praying for me as promised and then the conversation came to a close.

We were in the last week of December so I went the following day to see the doctor as previously scheduled only to find out that the office is closed and will not be open until after the New Year. The pain and cramps in my belly was unbearable and at that time, I had not menstruated for several months. I was positive, however, that I was not pregnant because I had been trying unsuccessfully for seventeen years to have a child for my husband. Nevertheless, I went to bed reassured that God would deliver me somehow after the woman of God prayed for me and said I would be healed.

Ah! The following morning I was awoken by a puddle of water in my bed. I sprung up to see what could possibly be the cause of my bed being so wet and much to my surprise, I was lying soaked in a pool of my own blood. "Oh my God, What is this?! What could this be?" I screamed. In that split second, I remembered the prayer that was uttered for me the night before.

Friends, my daughter who I mentioned earlier was delivered from her spiritual pit and anxiously approached me New Year's Eve saying she wanted to be baptized. My Christian neighbors tried their best to discourage both her and myself, saying, she is only sixteen so she is not ready to live a Christian life and that she will not last. My daughter was determined, however, and she was baptized. Now I have the privilege to see her pulling down strong holds, pulling me closer to God, witnessing like a veteran, praying like a warrior and still going strong after one year and four months.

Also, to my utmost surprise I am now 3 months pregnant after trying for seventeen years.

No one can tell me that there is no God. I am convinced there is nothing too hard for him to do. His timing is not ours but He is waiting for us to come boldly to Him with our supplications and prayers. Truly there is power in prayer and it absolutely knows no distance. I attribute my healing and my daughter's salvation to the power of prayer. Blessed are those who have not seen but believed because I know that my deliverance came from God. There are times when God speaks prophetically through His vessels to reveal His will for our lives. We only need to be patient.

Sister Jasmine, words are not enough to say how grateful I am to you for your prayers. You are blessed and have been a blessing to others. Blessed are those who walk in His righteousness.

Testimony: Fornication Overdose

Every woman's dream is to get married to Mr. Prince Charming. And I was not excluded from that dream. I met this born-again Christian man to whom I was attracted to and I thought the feeling was mutual. We dated for a while and as time went by the relationship got stronger and we grew closer. We were both single, never been married and lived by ourselves in our own homes. He would frequently visit me on the weekends; we shared numerous stories about ourselves and continued to grow fond of each other with each passing day. His visits became more frequent and he would linger for longer periods of time.

One particular evening he pretended to fall asleep and when he awoke, he did not want to take the chance and go on the street at that hour (according to him) so I agreed to let him stay overnight. Another weekend came and as usual he stopped by. We ate and exchanged thoughts, and at this time, I became blind-sided with the possibilities that soon I will be a wife. I could not clearly see the setup or the consequences of the enemy's darts. All that I had previously learned about resisting the devil flew out the door without my consciousness or awareness.

I was a born-again Christian and one who was a very mighty and powerful tool in the hand of God until the unthinkable happened. I started sinking deeper and deeper in sin. I was not living right and became enveloped by fornication. This thing was so strong in my life and it held me bound and in captivity for a while. I knew it was not right and I wanted to let go but never knew how. It seemed as if all hope was gone and that I had forgotten about God. I even stopped going to church could not pray anymore. I felt like a fish out of water. But, how many of you know that when God has a calling on your life and has you for a particular purpose, you can go but so far. He will send out his anglers to catch you and bring you back to shore.

I was never comfortable. Restlessness, misery and guilt consumed me and I was alive but I felt dead. One day while I was at work I saw an older woman come into my work place selling some gospel CD's and she asked if I would like to buy one. I said I would love to but I do not have enough money. She said it's alright and that she would take what I have. So I gave her the little I had at the time. After a long hard day at work, I went home and was prompted to play the CD. See, I knew what it was to feel and have a relationship with God but I had lost that connection and was desperately searching to recapture those moments again.

The CD was titled *"Fear Not"* and while it was playing, I was convicted by the song sharing the same name as the title and the testimony of the singer. I started crying and was so overwhelmed with guilt but I heard a voice said, "Call the number on the back of the disc." I called but to no avail. I tried to call numerous times without success but sometimes I left many messages on an answering machine or to another woman for the singer of the CD. Finally, and for the last time, I decided to try calling again. I got the same woman but this time she gave me the number for the person with whom I really wanted to speak. I called the number and finally reached her. I started to tell her how much of a blessing her CD had been to me. After a brief conversation, I asked her to pray for me and she did. She cried with me counseled and encouraged me. While she was praying, I felt like I wanted to vomit so I went into the bathroom and yes I did throw up. Immediately I felt like I was one hundred pounds lighter. I felt so free! During the prayer session, I saw something lifting from off me and went straight across the street.

Who could it be but Jesus?

My sisters and brothers in Christ, I have proven what is written in the book of Isaiah; "You cannot put a live coal in your bosom and don't get burned." I learned the hard way but now I can stand flat-footed and declare victory through the power of prayer. I give God all the glory because of the great things He has done. Now the Holy Spirit is my guide and the head of my life. He is the captain of my ship. It has been four years and I am happy to report that I am fornication free. I have been set free and I am clean and delivered by the power of God through prayer. If I was set free; you too can become liberated from the bonds of fornication. Do not give up! You may not be where you should be in Christ but as long as you are willing to surrender your weakness and faults to him, He is more than able. He did it for me and He will do it for you.

You may be wondering what happened to the relationship; did we get married? No, we did not. He left with another woman. Was I hurting? Oh, yes! However, it was better to hurt then than now. God sees a million miles down the road ahead of us and He knows what is good for us. My dear reader, if you can identify with this situation and God chose to cut some ties and detach you from where you were previously tied, do not be angry with God. He has your best interest at heart. You are royalty and should be treated accordingly. Not every and anything can enter into the palace.

Anything that is done excessively to the point where you are not in control and it has the power to kill you physically or spiritually is an overdose. But, God is the detoxifier.

Sister Jasmine thank you for taking time out of your busy schedule to pray with me and break that strong hold in my in my life. I am overjoyed to have met you and proud to call you my spiritual mother. It is a pleasure to share my testimony so others will know they are not alone; all they have to do is seek reinforcement. May God keep you and give you strength to continue to do His work.

Prayer

Most righteous and forgiving God, the ruler of the universe your name is worthy to be exalted. Father as I read this chapter I realize that I am not alone in my struggles. Lord I thank you for intervening for my sister and I am now asking you to intervene on my behalf. Dear God my flesh gets in the way sometimes and becomes uncontrollable. Lord it sometimes feel as if I am helpless and hopeless. It pains my heart to know that I am desecrating my temple and sinning against you and yet you still protect and care for me. Father I am crying out for deliverance from the thorn in my flesh. Jesus son of the living God, deliver me from every residue of fornication and adultery I renounce and denounce every attachment from my partners. I divorce every illegal spiritual husband or wife in Jesus name. I rebuke every desire to feed the flesh. Master, help me to give up pleasing the flesh and start pleasing you in Jesus name. Amen

And he said unto me, my grace is sufficient for thee: Most gladly therefore will I rather glory in my infirmities, that the power of Christ may rest upon me.

Testimony: 17 Years to Life: Freed after 24 years.

As a teenager, I thought I had a monopoly on life. In my own eyes, I was so smart that no one could tell me anything; not my parents and certainly not my teachers. I thought I was invincible and jail was not for me neither could I get into trouble.

My mom was not afraid to reprimand and punish me with every chance she received. She cried night and day and warned me about the company of friends with whom I surrounded myself. She would often say, "Roy, you have a bright and promising future ahead of you. Please, I am begging you do not throw your life away. If you continue on this path you will end up in the wrong place." "Son there is greatness locked up on the inside of you." Once again, I thought to myself that she does not know what she is talking about. In my mind, she is old and we are young and clever.

One bright summer evening my friends ask me to accompany them to pick up something. As usual I went. After all, we always roll together and it is just another evening like any other. Oh my God! It was not an ordinary evening as I imagined. It was a drug robbery gone badly and someone lost his life. I was not the one who pulled the trigger but I was there which makes me an accessory to murder.

Now what do I tell mommy? She warned and scolded me, and oh my God what do I do now? Jesus, why did I not listen when mom was directing me to the right way? She was not old and stupid after all. It was me who is the stupid one. I was thinking to myself that I am now dead and that this is it for me; my life is now over. All of this was going through my mind like a rocket. I know I was a rebellious teenager who did not listen to teachers or my parents in spite of their numerous punishments. At the end of the trial, I was given a sentence of seventeen years to life, which meant that after serving seventeen years behind bars, I may or may not be eligible for a parole hearing. The parole hearing would then determine if I was fit to re-enter society.

It was now September 2003. After being incarcerated for nineteen years, I was transferred from the Fishkill Correctional Facility to the Arthur Kill Correctional Facility in Staten Island where I would face the parole board for the second time. Not too long after arriving at the new facility, I was called for that long awaited hearing in October. My hopes were up very high that this would be my final appearance but I was still nervous. I went to the hearing but they gave me another two years. So I was denied for the second time and I would not be up again for my third hearing until 2005. At each hearing, I was given two years to reappear. Wow! I was disappointed and discouraged but I kept holding on to Romans 8:28. I thought to myself, Gods' timing is perfect and He must know why He allows me to be here so long.

I thank God for my upbringing in the church even though I went astray and allowed the devil to use me. During my lonesome time, I found the strength to read the bible which drew me closer to God. I got the opportunity to reflect on what my mother was trying to teach me and what I was taught in Sunday school. I felt as though these childhood teachings gave me a head start on the knowledge, love, and power of God as well as His grace, mercy and compassion towards me. The geographical location of the new facility to which I was transferred enabled me to pick up all the radio stations in New York City. I had found a few enjoyable gospel stations that I liked and I listened to them frequently. After a while, my relationship with God became deeper and stronger and I felt a connection that I had really never felt before. Listening to the gospel stations was all that I had left to encourage me to keep holding on to hope while I awaited my third parole hearing.

The year 2005 has arrived! This will be my third hearing and my 22nd year behind bars. "Oh boy, what will my fate be this time?" I asked. I have prayed; I had requested prayer; I had collected reference letters from people with whom I worked with in the facility to prove to the interviewers that I had changed and would not be a menace to society. With all of that, I was still holding on to Romans 8:28 and kept reassuring myself that God is in control. As a routine, I headed down to the parole room, sat before the people with my fate in their hands and would you like to guess what transpired this time? Yes, I was denied for the third time. I was crushed and for the third time I felt disheartened and discouraged. Nevertheless, I continued to hold to Romans 8: 28.

Thank God, for those gospel radio stations that kept me sane with the encouraging words. Every Friday night there was a radio program called *"The Count Down"* hosted by the late Pastor Layton Smith. It was a very informative program and whenever Pastor Smith was touched by a testimony or a song, he would do everything in his authority to get that person on as a guest on his program. He was a selfless man. After listening to him for a while, I realized that once he saw an individuals' potential or that someone had a message, he tried to pull it out and promote the individual.

All of us, inmates, would rush to finish our chores; make sure everything was in order then we would rush to get to the radio. We gathered in a comfortable corner just to listen to Pastor Smith. We rarely missed that program. This particular night, Pastor Smith was playing a song Titled *"Fear Not"* followed by a testimony. I was touched immediately and I fell in love with the song. Come to think of it, we were all touched by the song and the testimony. I decided to write to the pastor for a copy of the CD, which I did several times without a response.

Prison policy says one cannot receive any CD's or cassette that had screws in it and even if it was sent, they would not deliver it to the inmate because all packages were searched. One afternoon I was lying down in my cell when I was called to the package room. I went and was given a bulky envelope. I could not wait; I opened it immediately. Wow! Oh my God! It was a cassette and a letter from Sister Jasmine. In the letter, she stated that the secretary from the Countdown radio program gave her my information and my request. She copied the song from the CD onto a cassette and only God knows how it got through to me because screws were in it and I am sure she did not know the prison rules. I was shocked and at a loss for words. For one, many times packages came for me with CD's and cassettes and they were returned or destroyed. How did that one got pass? Sister Jasmine became my big sister. We started corresponding by mail and her letters were extremely encouraging, extolling God and His power to the highest. Our password in prison was "Fear Not!" When things were not going well, we would often say to each other "Fear Not" God will see you through. And for me, that was my theme.

As 2007 arrived, this was to be my fourth hearing and I was told that the hearing was scheduled for December 2007. Three months seemed rather long, much longer than the twenty-two years I had already served. I remember sending a prayer request to Sister Jasmine explaining my situation and that this will be my fourth time going to seek my freedom. She responded in her letter saying "Fear Not!" "God is with you and this is the last time you are going for a hearing, it is already done in the spirit realm only to be manifested in the physical." "As a matter of fact", she said, "You will be called before December. It is done."

I was called in October. Compared to my three previous appearances, this time I was at peace. I could not explain it I just knew I was not nervous or pessimistic. I do not know what was going to happen but all I knew was that the peace I was experiencing was enough for me whichever way it was going to turn out. My date in October came, for which I was neither anxious nor excited after being rejected so many times. I was now immune to the rejection so I did not raise my expectation only to get it knock down. At the hearing, I was still experiencing the peace of God; in my mind, it went okay I was told I would hear from them by mail, as usual.

The decision letter came like any other but I refused to open it. One of my friends volunteered to open it for me then he started screaming. A few more guys took the letter from him, read it and joined in their screaming party. I suspected what it might have been but I stood there with a straight face. Finally, I looked at it, hurrah!!!! I was free after 24 years.

Sister Jasmine thank you for those written words of encouragement, your prayers, and ah, that *Fear Not* song. Because of your testimony, I am elated to share my own. When you told me you were doing a book on the power of prayer, I knew without a shadow of doubt that I had to be a part of that project, just to encourage someone else and let him or her know that God is standing by and He is able to do anything if we pray. My sister, keep on singing, praying and sharing your testimonies. I am overjoyed to have known you. Because you were a humble available vessel, I was kept by the power of God through you. Like Esther, you have entered into my life for such a time as this, to shake the prison bars, break the bonds, petition the Lord on my behalf and set the captive free. Thank you Jas.

Love Roy.

Dear reader, I am sure by now you are curious to know what transpired after he was granted parole. He mentioned that I encouraged him; maybe. But he is the one who encouraged me; there was never a complaint in any of his letters to me. He always sounded happy, mature and together in his thoughts. The attributes of God flowed through his writings. Many of my now favorite bible verses I learned from him. I will never forget this one.

"Psalm 119:71 says, "It is good for me that I have been afflicted that I may learn thy statues." He was a walking bible.

After Roy's release from the big facility, if my memory serves me well, he was held in a detaining center awaiting deportation. At the center he was privileged to make collect calls and oh boy did he call. I had the pleasure of meeting his mom and aunt by way of telephone as he had told them about our relationship. Unfortunately, Roy and I did not get the opportunity to meet in person. He was eventually sent back to his place of birth where we correspond frequently. He calls me big sister and I call him my little brother.

However bad it may seem, I believe he was not arrested but was rescued by God who hid him in prison from both himself and others in order to save his life. There are times when we refuse wisdom and correction and it results in us paying a dear price. It may be loss of life, health or freedom. Nevertheless, God will turn it around in your favor so you can fulfill your purpose and reach your destiny. Each of us was born with purpose imbedded inside of us. Additionally, God has a special assignment for all of us to accomplish; people that need our assistance, whether physically or spiritually and places for us to go. Whatever God has to allow to take place in our lives, for us to accomplish our assignment, He will allow it. Jonah was sent to Nineveh but he rebelled, disobeyed God and detoured from his assignment. You might have heard the story. Jonah was swallowed by a big whale, which took him back to the original destination where the Lord sent him.

You may have seen yourself or someone you know in this testimony, but I encourage you, hold on and do not give up. Keep on praying and believing: it may be long but it will not be forever. Roy lost his childhood; gave up twenty-four years of his freedom, missed proms, graduations and all the enjoyable things life has to offer. However, according to him he kept holding to Romans 8:28.

Romans 8:28 And we know all things work together for good to them that love the Lord and to them that are the called according to his purpose.

Reader you may have been scared on your journey but it is only a reminder of the pathway you took and the testament of your victory. Roy did not allow his scars to block his long-term vision, he remained still enough to know God. Moreover, he was confident that God would deliver him one way or the other. I refer to him as Roy to protect his identity.

Fear not, there is still power in prayer!

Prayer

My father which is in Heaven; glory, honor and praise to your name. Father your perfect will has been done in this young man's life and I am depending on you to do the same for my family. Lord, you said in the time of trouble I should call on you. Here I am Lord calling for you to be a shield, a buckler, a tower of strength and to deliver me and my family from both physical and spiritual prison. Lord be our judge, be our defensive lawyer, be our jury and overturn every spiritual verdict that has been handed down to us by the enemy who walks in darkness, the terror by night and the noisome pestilence. Father God, deliver us from their destruction and let not their plot manifest in our lives. Lord I ask this in Jesus name. Lord, our lives are in your hands, lead and direct us from this day forward in the mighty name of Jesus Christ. Amen.

Romans 8:28 And we know all things work together for good to them that love the Lord and to them that are the called according to his purpose.

Testimony: Surgery Cancelled

I hosted a live Radio program called *"The Dynamic Gospel Hour"* in New York, which aired every Sunday evening from 6 to 7p.m. In the summer of 2007, on one particular Sunday evening I was not really feeling myself; I was low in spirit but could not put my finger on a reason. I said to myself there is no way I can go on the air like this. I cannot project this spirit of heaviness, confusion and restlessness into the air waves and onto my listeners and was immediately prompted by the Holy Spirit to lay prostrate on the floor and pray. Reluctantly I began to pray. I say reluctantly because my flesh did not want to pray, neither did it want to do the program and apart from that I did not want to lay down on the dirty floor since I resented even walking on it with my shoes. I was only praying for five minutes but in my mind it seemed as if I was praying for a long time. I was still feeling down. With forty-five minutes to go before airtime, I had to command my flesh to line up with the spirit of God. I had to reprimand myself that had I been on the phone, my conversation would have been longer than five minutes so there should not be a problem now that I needed to pray.

I went back on the floor with determination and in pursuit of the power and the anointing of God. I forced myself into praying. While I was there, the Lord began to reveal to me some frightening things. He said, "Get a pen and piece of paper and write all that I am showing you; I want you to talk about them on the air." I did as I was instructed. My sisters and brothers, the things I saw were not a beautiful sight but I will not go into details except for the one relevant to this testimony.

It is now 6p.m. and the broadcast is taking place. The atmosphere was charged and conducive to the anointing of God. After the preliminaries for the program, I started repeating what the Lord revealed to me. One of which was, "There is a woman with a big belly looking as if she is 9 months pregnant with swollen feet; the Lord said no surgery." Immediately the on air phone line rang. It was a listener who said she was driving on her way home and was praying and asking God to send help for her friend Beverly. She further stated that as soon as she walked in her house and turned the radio on she heard me describing a woman's condition and the description fit her friend who was currently in the hospital. The doctors could not find what was wrong with her and at one point they said she was pregnant which was not so. Then she was told she has cancer which also turned out to be a false alarm. Her feet were indeed swollen and her complexion getting darker and darker so the doctors considered doing surgery. "Can you pray for her?" she asked. At this time Evangelist Vendrix Headley was sitting in the studio and we looked at each other but I started crying. I asked Vendrix to pray. She did. Then I understand why I was feeling down and discouraged earlier. Satan did not want me to get in the presence of God because he knows when one gets into God's presence shackles will be broken, captives will be set free, all curse will reverse and oppression will lose its stronghold.

After the radio program, I went home marveled and was reminiscing about the entire evening. My cell phone rang; it was the caller asking me to accompany her to the hospital the next day to pray for her friend Beverly. Without any hesitation, I said yes. The Lord began ministering to me on what to do. Early Monday morning, I left Queens where I was living to meet with her in the Bronx where Beverly was hospitalized. Wow! Did we face opposition, obstacles and delays! Left right and center one after the other. When we finally got to the door I took a glimpse of her and literally wanted to run.

When I entered Beverly's room, she was lying across the foot of the bed like a piece of clothing. Her eyes were the color of a ripe banana and her feet looked like any minute they would burst open. And Oh! not to mention her belly; It was as if she was carrying sextuplets and her complexion was like a black leather bag. Yes, she looked that bad. Fear went into overdrive while faith took the back seat; I was scared out of my clothes. Quickly I gained composure and started reminding myself that God did not give me a spirit of fear but He gave me love, He gave me power and He allowed me to be sober so that anything contrary must be the devil trying to intimidate me. God may have revealed the woman's situation so I could be of some assistance; remember He knew the end from the beginning of time.

The Lord told me to get a bottle of water, olive oil and a white handkerchief. When faith stepped back in the driver's seat, the young

126

woman who asked me to accompany her to the hospital introduced me to Beverly. I explained what was in my hand and let her know that they are only instruments (water, oil and a piece of cloth) and of themselves, have no power but with Christ, healing is inevitable. I asked her if she would like to accept Jesus Christ as her Lord and Savior and she says yes so I led her to Christ. I saturated the handkerchief with some of the olive oil and laid it across her belly. Then I poured some of the water from the bottle into a cup, put a cap of olive oil in it and gave her to drink. My partner and I both laid hands on her belly and prayed for her. Not even 30 seconds had elapsed when I immediately noticed a change in her. I thought for a moment that my mind was playing tricks on me or that my eyes were deceiving me so I looked at my partner and asked if she noticed anything. She said, "Yes! The yellowness from her eyes is gone and she is not so dark anymore. Her countenance had changed and she seemed livelier." That was exactly what I saw: an instantaneous transformation. Fear not, there is still power in prayer.

Approximately two minutes later, a hospital staff came to take Beverly for her x-rays but she was unable to go because she said she felt as though she wanted to vomit. Beverly sat at the side of the bed for a little while but was only spitting out slime. The staff that came for her was getting impatient because she wasn't really vomiting. After a short while, they were ready to go to the x-ray room. I asked the staff how long ago was she supposed to get the x-rays done. The nurse stated that they were supposed to be done from that morning but there were some delays. When God has a promise to fulfill, He will put mans plan on hold for as long as He chooses. The once weakened Beverly got up with vibrancy and walked to the stretcher. Her roommate looked at her with amazement and said "Beverly! You look different; you're not so black again." I wanted to laugh but I refrained. With a strong voice, Beverly said, "thank you, I feel better, it's God!"

As she was about to lay down, I heard her making a weird sound and gesturing signs with her hand as she pointed to her mouth. They could not bring the basin fast enough before she started vomiting on the floor. You cannot imagine the mess that she was bringing up. When the basin came, she vomited in it as well. It was about seventy five percent full of bloody water with the olive oil swimming on top. Fear came back to lace my thoughts and for awhile I succumbed to the fear. I found a corner of the room and stood there very tightly. Underneath my breath, I began to say, "God, you cannot send me over here for demons to kill me; cover me Jesus. Lord, please don't let them follow me home nor attach themselves to my car or my son." Oh boy did I pray. I had never applied the blood of Jesus so much over my life before. If the blood of Jesus Christ could run out, I would have finished it that day the way I used it while praying.

While Beverly was gone to get her x-rays, we stayed in the room, cleaned everything with olive oil, and changed her bed linen. We waited for her to come back so we could change her clothes and anoint her with oil as well. Nearly two hours had gone by while we were waiting. My partner was in the bathroom and I was sitting in the hospital room, then I heard my partner say, "I am not leaving! We are not leaving!" I asked her who she was talking to and she said, "This 'ole demon telling me we should leave; we got here in peace so we should leave in peace." Man was I frightened and certainly enough, fear came showering over me again. I said to her, "So come let's go!" "I'm not leaving," she yelled back. I, therefore, had no choice but to stay still. Shortly after, Beverly's daughter came and without saying good evening, she asked, "Where is my mom?" I did not respond so she repeated "Where is my mom?" I said, "Good afternoon to you too." She said, "Good afternoon, now where is my mom?" I told her and then she asked, "So who are you?" I answered, "A servant of God." It was now 3 hours later and Beverly was just coming back from getting the x-rays when her daughter saw her and exclaimed, "Oh my God! Oh my God! Mommy you look different, what happened?" With an even stronger voice, Beverly said, "its prayer!" as she pointed to both me and my partner and said, "They prayed for me." The daughter did not know how long we had been in the room or what had taken place earlier.

Beloved reader, there is nothing too hard for the omnipotent God to do. He did it for Beverly and He can do it for you and your family. Beverly came out of the hospital three days later and the swelling in her belly and feet was drastically reduced. There was no baby and no surgery. Do not tell me there is no God. He still hears and answers prayers! He still delivers and He still has His people who He can trust and depend on to carry out what needs to be done. Most importantly, He is still speaking to His people. Will you quit being so busy and listen? He rewards those that diligently seek Him and His work and power will manifest in the physical realm. Fear not! There is still power in prayer.

Prayer

Glory to your name Jehovah Raphe the God that heals. Lord, I extol you, I honor you, I adore you, and I revere you. Father there is none like you, there is none to compare to you and your works. Oh, God how excellent is your name above the entire earth. Lord your word said you reveal to redeem and surely you have revealed Beverly's situation to your servant to deliver her from the onslaught of the enemy. Daddy Jesus, place my name on the heart of someone to pray for me, strengthen me, uplift and encourage me in Jesus name. Amen

Dear Reader,

The next section entitled "38 Reasons for Unanswered Prayers" is an excerpt from my next book. Many believers pray with expectation only to find that their prayers go unanswered because of underlying sins that may be present in their lives or for other reasons that they are not aware. This book will help you uncover some of those unconscious errors and lead to a more fulfilling prayer life.

Chapter 14

38 reasons for unanswered prayers

He that covereth his sins shall not prosper: but whoso confesseth and forsake them shall have mercy. Proverbs 28:13

Have you been praying for years and cannot see the answers to your prayers? You may be a prayer warrior, an intercessor or just someone who loves to pray but have not seen any answers to your prayers or any visible response to the specific situations for which you have been praying for years. Sometimes we believe that a "big" sin is the reason why our prayers go unanswered not realizing that God looks at all sin, whether big or small, as sin. For this reason; when sin is present in our lives, no matter how small, it can be the reason for many unanswered prayers.

There are many things that we are not aware of that can affect our prayer lives. In my next book entitled *"38 Reasons for Unanswered Prayers,"* we take an in-depth look at some of the "small" sins believers unconsciously engage in that have dire effects on their prayers. Obviously there are far more reasons/sins than 38 so why did we choose this random number? The number 38 signifies slavery and bondage which is exactly one of the disadvantages attached to sin. Psalm 66:18 says that "If I regard iniquity [sin] in my heart, the Lord will not hear me. Let us examine ourselves hence getting to the root cause of our unanswered prayers. God is not the problem so it has to be within us.

STEALING: Have you ever unconsciously taken paper towels, garbage bags and other supplies from your workplace for personal use at home? How about something as small and contrite as staples? If you did not ask to take them, this is considered stealing because it was not yours. What about the excess money you received from the cashier at the store or the extra $20 from the bank that you never returned? Were you the one to punch your time card when you were not at work? Does the time on your time card match the time you actually showed up for work? How many times within your hours at work you take coffee breaks then end up in the bathroom on the cell phone?

> *Let him that stole steal no more: but rather let him labor, working with his hands the thing which is good, that he may have to give to him that needeth.*Ephesians 4:28

NOT HIS WILL: Many times we pray and badger God for something to satisfy our own fleshly desires not concerning with the side effects and the consequences. We fast and pray and we kick and scream and sometimes start to negotiate with God. While God is simply saying, son or daughter, that which you want will cause you more pain and sorrow than satisfaction and gratification. I have something better for you but you must wait.

> *God having provided some better things for us, that they without us should not be made perfect.*Hebrew 11:40

HOMELIFE: How do you treat your spouse? How do you speak to each other compared to the way you speak to your friends? Do you complement each other? What happens during and after an intense argument? Was there an apology or is there resentment that lingers day after day? Do you respect each other? How about intimacy, is that the only time you show affection and give attention? Is there a desire or indifference? What about the children do you make and spend time with them and honor their requests? If there is a negative answer to any of the above, there is need for repentance. You cannot effectively love, praise, and represent God or preach to others while your relationship at home is in turmoil.

> *For if a man know not how to rule of his own house, how shall he take care of the church of God?* 1Timothy 3: 5

> *If any man say, I love God, and hateth his brother, he is a liar: for he that loveth not his brother whom he hath seen, how can he love God whom he hath not seen?* 1John 4: 20

> *But if any provide not for his own, and specially for those of his own house, he hath denied the faith, and is worse than an infidel (unbeliever).* 1Timothy 5:8

IMATURITY: Would you allow your fifteen year old son to manage your finances? Or would you hand a toddler a hundred dollar bill? Most of the things we are praying for are already placed in trust for us but we are not mature enough to handle them. Both David and Joseph had an inclination in their early years of their future but did not walk in their calling until they were in their thirties. That's the same way God will not allow you to be a millionaire, a homeowner, a wife or a husband until you learn and show some sign of responsibility and faithfulness.

> *I have yet many things to say unto you, but ye cannot bear them now.* John16:12

DOUBT: The absence of faith and trust is doubt. Doubt gives birth to worry causing one to miss out on God's best. If you are praying for an answer, but have the slightest notion of doubt that your situation might not change then you have already given yourself an answer that it will not and your prayers are in vain. Doubting God's promises, His power and His ability to get things done in His time is very disappointing to

Him. In essence you are saying: God I do not trust you and I don't think you can manage this. Just because you cannot see it in the physical or understand it in the spiritual, this doesn't mean it's bigger than God.

Trust in the Lord with all your heart; and lean not unto thine own understanding. Proverbs 3:5

Jesus said unto him, Thomas, because thou hast seen me, thou hast believed: blessed are they that have not seen, and yet have believed John 20:29

UNBELIEF: The absence of faith and the lack of belief is the plight of an unbeliever. When one disbelieves the word or the voice of God, they are already doomed. In order to receive from God you must believe His divinity: His death, burial and resurrection. Most importantly, you must believe His instruction manual, the bible. It is designed to keep us from making fatal mistakes while leading us along the path of righteousness. Unbelief opens the door for other sins to come in, take dominion and plant strongholds. If you refuse to believe that fornication is sin then you will continue to defile your temple which can eventually lead to diseases that will destroy your life as well. Unbelief lowers your spiritual credit score with God which results in an inability to receive. Sin is not unbelief but unbelief is a sin.

He that believeth on him is not condemned: but he that believeth not is condemned already, because he hath not believed in the name of the only begotten Son of God. John 3:18

FEAR: Fear is a feeling of agitation and anxiety caused by the presence or imminence of danger. This is the fear that is instrumental to our survival mechanism which alerts us of impending danger so we can protect ourselves. But, there is a kind of fear which causes us to be withdrawn, be inactive, have anxiety or cease from making progress. This fear means we are not depending on God or believing in His promise. Jesus told his disciples to "fear not" and "do not be afraid" 21 times. Fear is always found in the company of doubt and unbelief and can be very destructive when entertained. Fear is a thief that steals your joy, peace, dreams and potential. Fear is the opposite of faith because when a believer exhibits faith with determination, he or she can move mountains and every challenging situation must become subjected to the power within.

> *Fear not, for I am with you; be not dismayed, for I am your God. I will strengthen you, Yes, I will help you; I will uphold you with my righteous right hand.* Isaiah 41:10NKJ

BLASPHEMY AGAINST THE HOLY SPIRIT: The word blasphemy has many definitions, one of which is; "to speak evil of." It is mentioned 59 times in the New Testament all indicating that this sin is committed by the tongue, it's a mouth problem. If you blaspheme, (speak evil against) God or Jesus or the angels you will be forgiven. On the other hand, if you blaspheme (speak evil against) the Holy Ghost criticizing his manifestation in a derogatory way, comparing his work to that of a psychic or a witch there will be no forgiveness for you. It does not matter if you are a master prophet or your discernment is stronger than Elijah's, or you work more miracles than Jesus. To blaspheme against the Holy Spirit means that everlasting damnation will be your portion.

> [31] *Wherefore I say unto you, All manner of sin and blasphemy shall be forgiven unto men: but the blasphemy against the Holy Ghost shall not be forgiven unto men.*
>
> [32] *And whosoever speaketh a word against the Son of man, it shall be forgiven him: but whosoever speaketh against the Holy Ghost, it shall not be forgiven him, neither in this world, neither in the world to come.* Matthew12: 31-32

REJECTION: I was hungry, thirsty, naked, imprisoned and you neglected me. Every un-confessed sin in our lives is caused from rejecting the teachings of Jesus Christ. Rejecting God's unconditional love through his act of unselfish death for us means we reject Him as the supplier. We reject prayer, worship, assembling with each other and we reject the command to Seek God first.

> *For rebellion is as the sin of witchcraft, and stubbornness is as iniquity and idolatry. Because thou hast rejected the word of the Lord, he hath also rejected thee from being king.* 1Samuel 15:23

> *But whosoever shall deny me before men, him also will I deny before my father which is in heaven.* Matthew.10:33

> *Whoso stoppeth his ears at the cry of the poor, he also will cry himself, but shall not be heard.* Proverbs.21:13

HOMOSEXUALTY: The American psychological Association says that "Homosexuality is not a mental disorder and thus there is no need for a cure." I too agree that it is not a mental disorder and therefore cannot be physically treated. I believe homosexuality is a spiritual attack on God's creation and thus there is a need for deliverance. Many homosexuals say they were born that way but I beg to differ. In my opinion, there was a spiritual interference instigated by Satan and his demons somewhere between conception and delivery whether in the womb or through the birth canal. Many practice this behavior out of curiosity while some are confused and are struggling to identify with their identity.

Still, there are some who have encountered tragic sexual experiences such as rape or even betrayal from their heterosexual relationship and as a result, choose to enter into this lifestyle. It is important to note that God loves everyone, despite their sexual preferences but He hates your immoral sinful deeds. Like any other sin, homosexuality carries with it a death penalty if there is no repentance.

> [25] *Who changed the truth of God into a lie, and worshipped and served the creature more than the Creator, who is blessed for ever. Amen.*

²⁶ For this cause God gave them up unto vile affections: for even their women did change the natural use into that which is against nature **(lesbian)**

²⁷ And likewise also the men, leaving the natural use of the woman, burned in their lust one toward another; men with men working that which is unseemly, and receiving in themselves that recompence of their error which was meet. **(gay)**

²⁸ And even as they did not like to retain God in their knowledge, God gave them over to a reprobate mind, to do those things which are not convenient; Romans1:25-28

Also reference 1Corinthians 6:9-10 & Leviticus 18:22

If a man also lie with mankind, as he lieth with a woman, both of them have committed an abomination: they shall surely be put to death; their blood shall be open on them. Leviticus 20: 13

UNGRATEFULNESS: After all that was done for you and to you, you behave as if the individual was obligated to do what they did. You never say thanks. You never show your appreciation. But instead you find fault with the things that were done and murmur and complain about those that did not go your way. You tend to forget kindness and the sacrifices made for your comfort and wellbeing. You have forgotten the countless benefits you received.

How shall we escape, if we neglect so great salvation; which at the first began to be spoken by the Lord, and was confirmed unto us by them that heard him. Hebrew 2: 3

MURMURING: This is similar to the sin of ungratefulness; murmuring and complaining ties the hand of God causing Him to get angry and take drastic measures. No matter how many times you have seen God come through for you and working things out in your favor, you still find reason to complain. One minute you rejoice about His goodness and the next second you are asking, God where are you? Why me Lord? I cannot take it anymore. Give thanks in whatever situation you find yourself. God does not suffer from dementia so He knows what you are in need of and when you need it.

> [34] *And the Lord heard the voice of your words, and was wroth and sware, saying,* [35] *Surely there shall not one of these men of this evil generation see the good land, which I sware to give unto your fathers.* Deuteronomy 1:34-35

> *Neither murmur ye, as some of them also murmured, and were destroyed of the destroyer.* 1Corinthians 10:10

RESENTMENT: This is an attitude that seems insignificant but if left unattended is like adding fuel to fire. Resentment usually occurs from hurt. It's best if a hurtful situation is dealt with immediately so you can feel better without allowing bitterness to develop. Bitterness ruins relationships and trigger more dangerous sins like anger, hatred, and murder (etc.) It is possible to be angry and sin not but it is impossible to resent someone and be sinless. The heart of forgiveness is getting rid of resentment.

> [14] *Follow peace with all men, and holiness, without which no man shall see the Lord.*

> [15] *Looking diligently lest any man fail of the grace of God; lest any root of bitterness springing up trouble you and thereby many be defile;* Hebrew 12: 14-15

WAVERING: Wavering signifies uncertainty; lack of faith, instability, and double mindedness. A person who wavers tends to be confused and rarely makes conscious decisions. They will take one step forward and ten steps backwards because wavering has paved the way for fear, doubt, and unbelief to attack. Do not be mistaken and believe that when you waver you are being humble; you are dishonoring and discrediting God.

> ⁶*But let him ask in faith, nothing wavering. For he that wavereth is like a wave of the sea driven with the wind and tossed.*

> ⁷*For let not that man think that he will receive anything of the Lord.* James 1: 6-7

SELFISHNESS: Selfishness is a debilitating sickness. It definitely comes with readily identifiable symptoms; which are usually uttered in phrases like "Me", "Myself" and "I." Sadly, it is the family of the selfish individual that usually suffers the most because a selfish person rarely has the time to call or spend time with their loved ones. They are usually too busy pre-occupied with their own schedules to care enough to consider someone else's time. Apart from withholding food or money, selfishness comes in various packages.

Sometimes, even those who mean well behave selfishly without being conscious of what they are doing. A simple example is refusing to give someone a ride in your car. If you show no interest in other people's problems or tend to converse more about yourself than listen to the needs or concerns of others then you are behaving selfishly. Withholding information that can help someone else is also selfish. While you hate being interrupted or talked down to, you are being inconsiderate of someone else's feelings by saying mean things, interrupting what they are doing or saying to get your point across. This too is selfishness.

> *Do nothing out of selfish ambition or vain conceit. Rather, in humility value others above yourselves.* Philippians 2:3 NIV

SUBSTITUTING GOD'S WORD: God's word is yea and amen. Every word written in the bible is for us to obey and not to be twisted to fit our situation. God reminds us in Revelations 22:18-19 that if we add to his words plagues shall be added to us and if we take away from his words our life shall be taken out of the book of life. Many believers today distort the Ten Commandments for their convenience; sadly, they are unable to adhere to all of them so they say it is no longer valid and that we now live by grace. Do not forget: God does not change and before one of His written words become invalid heaven and earth shall pass away.

> *He that turneth away his ears from hearing the law, even his prayer shall be abomination.* Proverbs 28: 9

If you love me, keep my commandments St. John 14: 15

CRITICISM: Being critical of each other is wrong. Criticism is so rampant among churchgoers today. One can almost guarantee or expect to be criticized for something. Maybe it's the way you dress or the way you sing or preach. Sometimes you are criticized for being too quiet or too talkative. You can be criticized for driving a nice car or even if you are using your God given gift and talent to build the kingdom of God. Love speaketh no evil and criticism is the opposite of love; it is a sin. You will never know how criticism can leave lasting and devastating effects on an individual's feelings so do not engage in it as it may cause him to harbor resentment and anger.

> *Then said he unto his disciples, It is impossible but that offences will come: but woe unto him, through whom they come.* Luke 17: 1

WRONG MOTIVE: Why do we really do what we do? Is it to be seen or heard? Do you want a pat on the shoulder, praise, to be esteemed or to get glory? Or is it just so you say, "I've done that too" If you always want to hear how good of a job you are doing or seek praise for favors you render or brag on gifts you give then it is possible that you are doing with the wrong motive. It's different if you are sharing a testimony. But if you are constantly saying "I did this or I did that or had it not been for me" is sending the message that it was done out of the wrong motives.

When you ask, you do not receive, because you ask with wrong motives, that you may spend what you get on your pleasures.
James 4:3 NIV

¹*Take heed that ye do not your alms before men, to be seen of them: Otherwise ye have no reward of your father which is in heaven.*

³*But when thou doest alms, let not your left hand know what your right hand doeth.* Matthew 6:1& 3

LYING: Are the children you claimed on your taxes yours? Do you really spend all you are claiming? What is the real reason why you are late for work or called in sick? Is your excuse for not being in church the truth? Is the information on the job application or the lease application the truth? These are some of the things we lie about and they seem so insignificant and harmless that we forget to repent. In my opinion, it is better to be poor and have relationship with God rather than to lie and lose that opportunity.

⁹*A false witness shall not be unpunished, and he that speaketh lies shall perish.*

²²*The desire of a man is his kindness: and a poor man is better than a liar.* Proverbs 19: 9, 22

UN-FORGIVENESS: Many times we say we forgive but that is far from the truth. If there is tension when you are around the person with whom you have an issue or feel awkward to participate in their conversation or even to respond when they say hello, it's a tell-tale sign that the issue is unresolved. Say for example, you find yourself at an event and the individual with whom you had the issue is also at the same event. If you feel at this point that your evening is ruined and you start experiencing anger when the memory of the hurt comes back, it simple means that there is still a soreness which you have not forgotten and it is not forgiven. At the end of the day, you are the one hurting, being un-comfortable and having sleepless nights. Even though you may not forget it, it is best to forgive and put it behind you so that your healing process can begin. Forgiveness does not mean you forget the circumstances surrounding your hurt or even to place yourself back in the same position to get hurt again; it just means that you are freeing yourself of excess and unnecessary pain. Most importantly, as your heavenly father forgave you of many indiscretions, you are also following His example to forgive your earthly brothers and sisters.

> [14] *For if ye forgive men their trespasses, your heavenly Father will also forgive you:*
>
> [15] *But if he forgive not men their trespasses, neither will your Father forgive your trespasses.* Matthew 6:14-15

BITTERNESS: Un-forgiveness is usually the root cause for bitterness. If you find yourself harboring bitter feelings towards your neighbor or find that your tone is very sharp or resentful whenever you are around someone that you have not forgiven, bitterness is usually the underlying culprit. Sometimes bitterness lends itself to severe dislike which eventually turns to hatred. For example, you might find yourself being very disagreeable or cynical to the suggestions or ideas that come from the individual whom you dislike. Finally, if you would move mountains to seek revenge or cause sorrow and pain to the individual that hurt you then you are indeed consumed with bitterness.

> *Let all bitterness, and wrath, and anger, and clamour, and evil speaking, be put away from you, with all malice:*
> Ephesians 4: 31

ANGER: In my opinion, anger is a deeply embedded emotion that is either brought on by something or someone else. But even though the latter is true, anger is still an emotion that an individual chooses to entertain or harbor. Anger, is however, curable. Getting to the heart of our emotions and ultimately the causes that make us angry can help us regain control of our emotional lives and our temperaments. Perhaps your anger stems from some tragic incident; a rape from a family member; rejection from your parents, rejection from your spouse or even your children. Sometimes those incidents are inflicted by church members or people with whom you have placed your earnest trust. May-be your anger stems from being raped or mistreated during childhood or lack of attention during childhood and even in your adult years. Whatever the cause of your anger, you will need to address it or you will find yourself lashing out on everyone and everything because that initial source of anger was not addressed. Gaining control of one's emotional state of mind means to gain enjoyment in one's life and living it to its fullest.

> *"But I tell you that anyone who is angry with a brother will be subject to judgment."* . . . . _{Matthew 5:22 NIV}.

> *Refrain from anger and turn from wrath; do not fret—it leads only to evil.* _{Psalm 37: 8 NIV}.

> *Do not be quickly provoked in your spirit, for anger resides in the lap of fools.* _{Ecclesiastes.7: 9 NIV}

COVETOUSNESS: The sin of covetousness is one of the most subtle and dangerous sins that no one really speaks or preaches about these days. But, unbelievably, it is a sin that competes with God for our hearts, which makes Him angry. It is the foundation for envy, jealousy, uncontrollable greed and strong lustful desire for money and material gain. Covetousness motivates one to commit murder, work witchcraft, and to get involved with pornography, prostitution, which eventually assassinates his or her character. Covetousness stems from lust: your eyes have seen it so now you must have it no matter the cost or the consequence.

Thou shalt not covet thy neighbor's house, thou shalt not covet thy neighbor's wife, nor his manservant, nor his maid servant, nor his ox, nor his ass, nor anything that is thy neighbor's.
Exodus 20:17

[1]What causes fights and quarrels among you? Don't they come from your desires that battle within you? [2]You desire but do not have, so you kill. You covet but you cannot get what you want, so you quarrel and fight. You do not have because you do not ask God. James 4: 1-2 NIV

JEALOUSY: Jealousy is the off spring of envy. It is an irrational behavior compounded with pain, sadness, low self-esteem and inferiority; always wanting to have what someone else has or to do what someone else does in a negative, competitive, deceptive and undermining way. If at first glance, you cannot sincerely compliment an individual on their accomplishments or possession but rather first saying something negative or sarcastic, then that is a sign of jealousy. "I can do it better, I must have that too, you are just showing off, or it doesn't take all that." If these words are found in your vocabulary, either the jealousy bug bites you or its just plain bad mindedness.

Anger is cruel and fury overwhelming, but who can stand before jealousy? Proverbs 27:4NIV

ENVY: Envy is not a new kid on the block; it has been in existence since creation. It is the strongest and most dangerous. In fact, Isaiah 14:12-14 accounts for the seven behaviors Satan exhibited. As the scripture notes, Satan was not kicked out of heaven because of pride but because of covetousness, which made way to envy, then gave birth to the spirit of pride. When pride takes control, it is very difficult for an individual to submit to Gods authority. If you are feeling a sense of discontent with your position and possession and strongly desire another's property by any means necessary, even by murder, you are exhibiting the spirit of envy. Where envying and strife is there is confusion and every evil work.

> *A heart at peace gives life to the body, but envy rots the bones.*
> Proverbs 14:30.NIV

DISOBEDIENCE: Many times we sin against God by disobeying His words. We then justify our behavior by declaring that we are living under the dispensation of grace, thus taking advantage of its benefit. Thou shalt not tempt the Lord thy God. What was your response when God gave you a command not to do something? Did you marry someone that God said is not your husband or wife? How did you react when God told you to wait? What have you done with the money that God gave you to put aside? Disobedience is the first and last sin. It will cost us our inheritance if we do not identify it and repent.

> *Know ye not, that to whom ye yield yourselves servants to obey,*
> *his servants ye are to whom ye obey; whether of sin unto death,*
> *or of obedience unto righteousness.* Romans 6:16

CORRUPT COMMUNICATION: Communication is verbal and nonverbal. It has the power to uplift, tear down, persuade, manipulate, convert, and influence. As such, believers must be weary at all times and sharply alert. Do not forget that the conception of good and evil begins in the mind. After your mind has entertained certain ideas for awhile, it then gives way for your mouth to voice it, giving birth to the idea. For example, a telephone conversation might begin very simple but two hours later after reminiscing on the past; you might find yourself swearing or using profanity. Another trap that plagues Christians is their willingness to accept sexual compliments, not realizing that it segues into many unwanted temptations whether in the form of adultery or fornication. It is imperative for believers to be mindful of their speech because it can often take them down a pathway that was never intended.

Let no corrupt communication proceed out of your mouth, but that which is good to the use of edifying, that it may minister grace unto the hearers. Ephesians 4:29

MALICE: I thought malice means not talking to an individual but Webster defines it as a desire to harm, ill will. Follow me closely if indeed you really have an evil intention and a desire to hurt someone that means you hate and despise that person, Therefore, not talking to an individual would be the first stage of that evil intent, in other words malice would be the result of the build-up in the human pipeline overtime.

Wherefore laying aside all malice, and all guile, and hypocrisies, and envies, and all evil speaking, 1Peter 2:1

PRIDE: What is pride? Sinful pride is one of seven most deadly sins that God hates. Pride is similar to a disease in which the carrier is unaware that he or she has been infected. Pride is conceited, inconsiderate and selfish. An individual that is filled with pride always seek to impress, craves attention, marvels to center of attraction, always want to be acknowledged and praised for the tasks they do and complains if they don't get things done his or her way. Pride likes to exalt him or herself above others. Sometimes it is done under a guise of generous giving, just so the individual can say I did this or I did that. But, where help is truly needed, they murmur and complain because they were not the one who initiated the act.

Prideful people seek to usurp authority and refuse to be corrected especially by someone who they feel is beneath them. They are easily offended but are quick to offend others. They play the role of what I call the "Holy Ghost police" because they readily point out others' faults, weaknesses and mistakes without first acknowledging their own. They appear to be perfect and disciplined on one hand but on the other hand, they despise the fact that someone is more influential, powerful, effective, or even more intelligent than they are. Humble yourself under the mighty hand of God; He will exalt you in due season.

For if a man thinks himself to be something, when he is nothing, he deceiveth himself. Galatians 6:3KJV

But let every person carefully scrutinize and examine and test his own conduct and his own work. He can then have the personal satisfaction and joy of doing something commendable [in itself alone] without [resorting to] boastful comparison with his neighbor. Galatians 6: 4 Amplified version

TALE-BEARING: The tongue is an unruly evil full of deadly poison; it cannot be tamed. A tale-bearer continually uses his or her mouth to damage the reputation or character of others. Whenever someone confides a secret in your trust, it must be kept to yourself. Instead, a tale-bearer will pick up the phone and start calling all of his or her friends to say, "Guess who got a divorce?" or "Did you hear about Tony?" Even though it may be the truth, it is a betrayal of trust. What's worse is a tale-bearer usually sows seeds of discord. Where there is no tale-bearer there is no strife. Psalms 50:16-21 references the tale-bearers judgment.

[16]But to the wicked, God says: what right do you have to recite my laws or take my covenant on your lips? [17]You hate my instruction and cast my words behind you. [18]When you see a thief, you join with him; you throw in your lot with adulterers. [19]You use your mouth for evil and harness your tongue to deceit. [20]You sit and testify against your brother and slander your own mother's son.[21] When you did these things and I kept silent, you thought I was exactly like you. But I now arraign you and set my accusations before you. Psalms 50: 16-21 NIV

He that covereth a transgression seeketh love; but he that repeateth a matter separateth very friends. Proverbs 17: 9 KJV

BACKBITING: Backbiting, gossiping, tale-bearing, and slander are all abominable diseases inflicted by the tongue that God hates. A backbiter talks negatively with evil intentions about another person or their "friend" or an associate behind his or her back to tarnish the individual's reputation. Then, staying true to their deceptive form, they smile and pretend as if innocent when they are in front of the individual whom they have just maligned. This behavior happens so frequently that it seems like a practiced norm. Or, perhaps we have seared our conscience by ignoring the fact that we do this often without feeling some sort of sensitivity to the issue. Be careful of the one who says, "Let us pray for Joe" but then proceed to disclose all of Joe's business or personal matters. These individuals who pretend to care can easily be discerned by not what comes out of their mouth but the size of their heart. Do their actions match what they say? Do they honestly care about or are considerate towards the person whose business they are readily willing to broadcast? Do not allow anyone to turn you into a gossiper or an outlet for negative news. Protect your mouth and ear gate! Use your tongue as an instrument for blessing and restoration.

> *¹Lord, who shall abide in thy tabernacle? who shall dwell in thy holy hill? ²He that walketh uprightly, and worketh righteousness, and speaketh the truth in his heart. ³He that backbiteth not with his tongue, nor doeth evil to his neighbor, nor taketh up a reproach against his neighbor.* Psalms 15: 1-3

IDLE TALK: The New Living Translation version of Proverbs 10:19 says, "Too much talk leads to sin. Be sensible and keep your mouth shut." This means that when there are too many unnecessary words spoken, one tends to talk out of context, blurt out loose words and therefore starts to exaggerate stories. The New Testament book of James calls the tongue an "evil poison." David said he will guard his ways and restrain his mouth with a muzzle that he might not sin with his tongue while in the presence of the wicked (ungodly). Sadly, when we are in the company of unbelievers who tell profane jokes and stories, we laugh and give our input not realizing that we are entertaining an unacceptable behavior. This makes us an accessory to what they are doing or saying. We may not voice it ourselves but our mere participation in it makes us just as guilty. It is very easy to pick up and repeat bad habits if not careful. Take control of your tongue and watch what you say!

> *Nor should there be any obscenity, foolish talk or coarse joking, which are out of place, but rather thanksgiving.* Eph. 5:4 NIV

> ³⁶*But I say unto you, that every idle word that men shall speak, they shall give account thereof in the day of judgment.* ³⁷*For by thy words thou shalt be justified, and by thy words thou shalt be condemned.* Matthew 12:36-37NIV

DECEPTION: Deception is the sin of misleading by a false appearance or statement. It is so cunning that it is not really telling a blatant lie but making a statement or withholding key information which misleads an individual into believing something else. It is an appearance of the truth but farthest from the reality of the truth. Deception comes from the word deceit in which is defined as lying, fraud, cheating and mystification. It is the intention to conceal, camouflage, and distract. Deception violates trust and gives birth to feelings of betrayal and anger.

> ¹⁷ *I urge you, brothers and sisters, to watch out for those who cause divisions and put obstacles in your way that are contrary to the teaching you have learned. Keep away from them.* ¹⁸*For such people are not serving our Lord Christ, but their own appetites. By smooth talk and flattery they deceive the minds of naïve people.* Roman16:17-18 NIV

IDOLATRY: Idolatry is the act of worshiping your possessions, or an image or other things and allowing them to take preeminence in your life. Moreover, you have given them permission to take the place of God in your heart. An idol is that which you give excessive devotion and reverence, and forgetting God. An idol may be in the form of a person, your job, house or car. As absurd as it may seem, doing the work of God can consume you to the point where it becomes your idol causing you to miss God and His purpose for you. Can you imagine someone saying, "I don't get much time to spend with God because of my job?" Or "I can't find the time to go to church for 2 hours because I only get one rest day and I have to mow my lawn; paint my house; wash my car and spend time with my kids." Anything that consumes your time or takes you away from your time with God is an idol in your life. Consume your idol before it consumes you!

> *Do not turn away after useless idols. They can do you no good, nor can they rescue you, because they are useless.* 1 Samuel 12: 21 NIV

> [12]*I will expose your righteousness and your works, and they will not benefit you.* [13]*When you cry out for help, let your collection of idols save you! The wind will carry all of them off, a mere breath will blow them away. But whoever takes refuge in me will inherit the land and possess my holy mountain.*
> Isaiah 57: 12-13NIV

WITCHCRAFT: Witchcraft is the malicious evil works by witches, warlocks, necromancers and other satanic agents. Their intention is to kill, deform or frustrate and confuse the life, mind and body of another human being through evil (demonic) spirits. Witchcraft is one of the satanic magical powers used by humans (Satan's agents/ employees) to cast spells, manipulate and gain earthly and supernatural power and wealth without submitting to God. It is a form of idolatry and deception with the intent to control territories, government, people, marriages, religions and much more. Unfortunately, many Christians practice witchcraft unaware. For example, some believers may find it entertaining to read what their horoscope says and get caught up in astrological and zodiac signs. They eagerly call psychic hot lines or burn candles or go to palm/ tarot card readers. Do not be deceived, there is no good witch or good magic!

[11]And I will cut off the cities of thy land, and throw down all thy strongholds: [12] And I will cut off witchcrafts out of thy hand; and thou shalt have no more soothsayers: Micah 5:11-12

SORCERER: An individual who is assisted by demonic spirits or fallen angels to carry out and exercise magical powers to which they refer to as beneficial magic. They use this to assist them in gaining power so they can intimidate and interfere with the will and mind of innocent people and tamper with their possessions. They seek to usurp authority. But I see them as weak, desperate, double minded and ungrateful people wanting to become god. They deceive people into believing they can heal and deliver them from sickness or oppression when in fact they cannot. What they do is assign a higher ranking demon to the individual to keep the oppressing demon quiet for a while. Things appear calm as if their professed "healing" works but shortly after, it starts to get chaotic because it is not a part of their character to do good. You cannot bargain with the devil; you will always be on the losing side. Much the same way that a kingdom divided against itself cannot stand. If we seek God, put our trust in him and arm ourselves with His word, we can overpower and destroy the powers of darkness.

[11]Therefore shall evil come upon thee; thou shalt not know when it riseth: and mischief shall fall upon thee; thou shalt not able to put it off: and desolation shall come upon thee suddenly, which thou shalt not know.

[12]Stand now with thy enchantments, and with the multitude of thy sorceries, wherein thou hast laboured from thy youth; if so be thou shalt be able to profit, if so be thou mayest prevail.

[13]Thou art wearied in the multitude of thy counsels. Let now the astrologers, the stargazers, the monthly prognosticators, stand up, and save thee from these things that shall come upon thee. Isaiah 47:11-13

REBELLION: Rebellion is a willful act of disobedience. With an already made up mind, you insist on going ahead with your plans no matter what the consequence with total disregard for instruction or direction. One who exhibits a stubborn attitude with the notion of "it's their way or no way" is held captive by the spirit of rebellion. You are purposely telling God, "I heard you but I will not obey and I do not care what you want to do because I am going to please my flesh."

> *For rebellion [disobedience] is as the sin of witchcraft, and stubbornness is as iniquity and idolatry. Because thou hast rejected the word of the Lord, he hath also rejected thee from being King.* 1 Samuel 15:23

HYPOCRISY: Hypocrisy is the manifested action of a hypocrite; one who acts self-righteous, always believing that they are holier or more perfect than everyone else. In their eyes, their sin is not as bad as the other person and their wrongs are justified. If you find yourself condemning someone for the same behavior you are exhibiting or if you are preaching one thing and living another then you are a hypocrite. Furthermore, if you instruct or ask an individual to do a task then you do the total opposite or hold yourself to different standards then you are in fact a deliberate hypocrite. Deliberate hypocrites run ranks with deceivers, pretenders and are no better than the Pharisees whom Jesus cursed.

> *³So you must be careful to do everything they tell you. But do not do what they do, for they do not practice what they preach.*
>
> *⁴They tie up heavy, cumbersome loads and put them on other people's shoulders, but they themselves are not willing to lift a finger to move them.* Matthew 23: 3-4 NIV.

GLUTTONY: The dictionary defines a glutton as a person who eats or drinks excessively. The bible calls gluttony a sin. And if it is a sin, like any other sin, it is driven by a spirit. In my opinion, a demonic spirit of suicide influences gluttony. Ponder it for a moment. Oppressive spirits causes you to overeat and consuming more than is needed for the body to function leaves the door open to self-debilitating diseases like diabetes, high blood pressure, heart attack or stroke caused by blocked arteries due to a build-up of cholesterol. If you find yourself constantly eating, even when you are not hungry, or spending your last dime on food that you do not really need or getting up various hours at night to raid the refrigerator, you are possessed with the spirit of gluttony. Have you ever seen someone eating something and all of a sudden, you start craving for it?

Gluttony is named as one of the seven most deadly sins. Solomon says if you are a man given over to your appetite, you should put a knife to your throat. This should be one of the perfect reasons to fast. Starve that demon to death and gain self-control. With God, all things are possible.

> [20]*Do not join those who drink too much wine or gorge themselves on meat,* [21]*for drunkards and gluttons become poor, and drowsiness clothes them in rags.* Proverbs 23: 20-21NIV

Perhaps you are looking for more explanations on other sins or asking why a particular sin was not mentioned. I did not mention them because you already know what they are. Therefore, be careful not to commit them and if you do, repent immediately! Most of the sins in the aforementioned paragraphs are regularly ignored and committed without remorse. They are synonymous to the analogy of the straw that broke the camels' back. By itself, one straw does not seem like a lot, in much the same way a small sin does not seem like sin. But they are sins nonetheless and in actuality can become a very heavy weight if not dealt with from its beginning stages. For example, you readily know that lying and stealing is a sin but you were probably not thinking that taking something as small as staplers home from work without asking is in fact stealing. Since you are not thinking that these are sins, you are probably not asking forgiveness either because you believe these are small innocent actions. But they are not just small and innocent because if they are committed without repentance then there is no reconciliation with God. If there is no reconciliation then there is no salvation and if no salvation then everlasting damnation shall be your portion. This is the everlasting mystery that perplex believers and stagnate their prayers because they have un-reconciled sins in their lives that have not been addressed.

It is my earnest prayer that as believers, you are more watchful, alert and aware of the things that cause you to sin. And, if you commit a sin do not hesitate to repent. The adversary is conscious of the fact that he will not be able to devour everyone but he knows that there are those who will consciously leave doors open and unconsciously give him permission and easy access to create a stronghold that will take dominion and authority over your life. This is why the devil prowls back and forth seeking. If at first he is not successful, he will come back again and again to see which door you have neglectfully left open. Do not leave any door or window open! Do not be his victim. PRAY!!!!

Prayer

Unto you oh God, I lift up mine eyes and my voice. I pray that you will hear me from within your Holy place. Lord, your word says that you do not hear nor answer a sinner's prayer unless it is the prayer of repentance. Therefore Lord, I come boldly before you asking forgiveness for all my iniquities and transgressions, my unrighteousness and sins as I name them one by one. Purge me thoroughly from sins of deception, gossiping, tale-bearing, backbiting, hypocrisy, disobedience and rebellion. Heavenly Father; like the eyes of the servant look unto the hand of his master and the eyes of the maiden look unto the hand of her mistress, so my eyes wait upon you for mercy and deliverance in Jesus name.

Merciful Father, I am guilty of lying and stealing. Lord for years I ignored these bad habits not knowing how detrimental they are to my prayers and my Christian walk. God I am guilty and I ask your forgiveness. Holy Spirit, I seek you right now for instant deliverance from the spirit of jealousy, covetousness, envy, malice, resentment and any wrong motive that may be inside of me. Father, for too long I have allowed these sins to hinder my spiritual growth and progress. Lord, teach me how to be sincerely happy and celebrate for my sisters and brothers when they have received of your blessings. Help me not to become jealous or envious so that I may in turn release my own blessings. Let me hold no grudge oh God but help me to adhere to your words so that none of these sins will be named in my life, in Jesus mighty name.

God, I am consumed with ungratefulness, bitterness, anger, un-forgiveness and pride. Cleanse me thoroughly oh God as I repent in your presence. These are the things which easily beset me and rob me from experiencing your joy and your peace. Mighty God I cast them all on you in exchange for your yoke that is easy and your burden that is light. Father, I acknowledge that I am full of pride and that my selfish attitude has blinded my eyes, causing me to reject your words and be inconsiderate to others. Master, from the bottom of my heart, I cry out for your help this day. God I am not living my best life because of this baggage that weigh me down. Holy Spirit, please re-arrange my mind and reconstruct my thoughts and teach me how to be humble in Jesus mighty name.

Deliverance! Deliverance! Oh God, I know your ears are not heavy where you cannot hear me and neither is your hand short that you cannot save me. Father, there are iniquities which stand in my way and prevent my prayers from being heard. Because of this, I cannot receive my breakthrough. Lord, I am held hostage by the spirit of hate, (I am or was) involved in a sexual lifestyle contrary to your words. I have unknowingly (or knowingly) been involved in witchcraft and sorcery, fornication, adultery and I am guilty of putting idols before you. I declare those chains broken and put them out of my life as I ask you to forgive me for abusing and destroying my temple. Forgive me God for putting other gods before you. Holy Spirit rid me from any residue or lingering fowl spirit that may try to lure me into practicing these sins again in the mighty name of Jesus.

Holy Spirit, I thank you for your mercies that are brand new every morning. I thank you for not giving me the punishment I deserve and I thank you for not leaving me as prey to the enemy. Thank you for not delivering me over to the hand of those who seek my life. Most of all, thank you for not taking your love or your spirit away from me. Lord I have deliberately walked in fear, unbelief and doubt. I have entertained corrupt communications, allowed idle words to proceed out of my mouth and murmured over everything that is not going my way. Lord, I have wavered and have gone against your words. Father I have blasphemed against you and your son's name but I beg you Jesus put a watch over my mouth and a bridle over my tongue that I may not blaspheme against the Holy Spirit. God let me keep my mouth shut if I do not understand or have anything good to say about the operation or the manifestation of the Holy Spirit. Lord I do not want to miss eternal life with you after sacrificing so much. These I pray in Jesus mighty name.

Omnipotent God, teach me how to take care and rule my home so that I will be able to take care of the church of God. Lord, I thank you for the responsibility to impact the lives of others so I ask you now to help me to lead your people in the path of righteousness. Master you know what is best for me so let me not ask for anything that is beneath me or will cause my destruction. Do not grant me any request to fulfill the desires of my flesh that will make me walk out of your perfect will. Help me instead to learn how to wait upon you. God, sometimes I behave so immaturely and become critical of others. I have even been critical of you Lord and have questioned your path and direction for me. Lord, I ask for your forgiveness and mercy in Jesus name.

Father God, gluttony has been categorized as one of the seven sins that you hate strongly. I rebuke the spirit of gluttony out of my life right now in Jesus name. Father God I realize and admit that my belly has become my god. I am over-indulging in foods that are causing my spiritual man to be ineffective and my physical body to suffer the consequences. Deliver me oh God from these unhealthy eating habits and take away my cravings and desires for unhealthy foods. Father, replace those yearnings with a consciousness to crave healthy foods and help me to stay motivated to engage in physical exercise. Lord I want to practice everything in moderation and maintain discipline to uphold this new way of eating in Jesus mighty name. Amen.

Chapter 15

A final thought

A Final Thought

Ten years ago, immediately after I was saved, I got the vision to write this book, "Fear Not! There is **STILL** Power in Prayer." I began on the journey to put on paper some revelations that the Lord had shown me, having no idea of all that would transpire and in which direction it will go or even how it will flow. Throughout the years, I paused from writing but continued to saturate myself with prayer, praise and worship which enabled me to gather the information that I share with you today. At one point I was told that I am so heavenly minded that I am no earthly good and that I needed a balance. Nevertheless, I persevered and was not deterred by negativity. I thought this project would have long been completed and available to the public but apparently it was not the right season. Now the fulfillment of time has come and I am finally able to share this message with you. It has been a journey but we have arrived.

Under the instruction of the Holy Ghost, this book is intentionally designed to reach the homes of the lonely, the heart of the broken, the mind of the confused and the life of those who seem hopeless. It is written to empower, educate, equip and encourage any and everyone to foster a relationship with God. In the process, you will learn the art and value of effective praying that will yield results. It will be rewarding to know that you can beat the enemy at his own game through the power of prayer.

Whenever you are challenged by the vicissitudes of life, prayer is the solution to neutralize and restrain the strong man that is at work. With "*still*" being the operative word in the topic of the book, I believe God wants you and I to know that He never stops answering prayers. Additionally, He wants to remind you that your prayer still has the power to change your circumstances. You should not be intimidated by the negative things that are happening around you. I encourage you to be patient in whatever task you undertake. Although my task took ten years to complete, this does not necessarily mean yours will take that long, as well as it can take longer. Either way, God knows the end result of a thing before it begins. In other words, if there are delays it is for a reason. Reasons that we may never know or understand.

The Importance of a Prayerful Life

Many of us find time to pray when we are in need of something. We ask the Lord to allow our interview to go well so we can gain employment. We ask Him for a husband or a wife or we ask Him for the funds to purchase a new car. We may even ask Him for spiritual gifts or even to be a better singer on the choir. Even though God welcomes our requests for our material and spiritual needs, He already knows what we need before we ask Him. Therefore, I want to encourage you to let your prayer lives be more than just for the asking. Instead, take your prayer life to a new level by building a relationship with God. Pray even when you don't need anything at the moment. Pray and thank the Lord just because you have the opportunity to freely converse with Him and because you cherish your relationship with Him. In turn, God will reward you openly. Be reminded, He will not withhold any good thing from His children. Furthermore, who wants to be in a one-sided relationship where the only time you communicate is when you are asking the other person for something. As humans, we do not feel good about such relationships, much the same way, God is not pleased when we only come to Him begging.

There are many unrequested rewards that the Lord grants freely without us even asking. Maintaining a prayerful relationship with the Lord has these unspoken benefits. For one, we live in a dangerous world and we are unaware of the impending turmoil that lay-wait us. But the Lord protects those that are His own. David said, "Yea though I walk through the valley of the shadow of death I will fear no evil for thou (God) art with me." It is not a matter of *if*; but *when* you face your valley experience, do not despise the valley regardless of how thick the debris may be or how heavy the waters that tumble down around you. The fact that God is with you always mean that no harm shall come near you. The purpose of the valley is not to destroy you; it serves as a teacher to make you stronger and to equip you to assist others who are going through their valleys and may not know how to cope. What's more, your valley experience allows you to appreciate your blessings when God brings restoration, comfort, reassurance, purpose and peace. Have you noticed that when we are in the valley, we want to seek more of God? Problems tend to draw us closer to Him and seek more of Him. The valley is the birthplace for miracles and revelation. It allows us to depend whole-heartedly on God. It is a set aside place for purging, pruning, processing and to eradicate pride from us. In addition, our praise is more genuine because we have a pressing issue so we have no choice but to look up to Him.

The valley is a pre-requisite for our success and elevation to the mountaintop as it is impossible to get to there without first being in the valley. Unfortunately, the mountaintop has its advantages as well as its disadvantages. Whenever we are on top, we are now more open and susceptible to haters who prey and try to devour us at every opportunity. On the mountaintop we are even susceptible to our own pride which can sometimes have devastating effects even more so than the hands of mortals. After our arrival on the mountaintop, some of us are caught posing instead of praising God for our breakthrough. As humans, we do have the tendency to brag about our accomplishments and if we are not careful, want to condescendingly look down on others as if to say they are beneath us or out of our league. When this type of attitude starts to develop, it means that we did not learn anything while being in the valley and therefore must return for a lesson in humility.

Remember it is human to succumb to the lusts of the flesh, the pride of life and temptation. But we overcome these through prayer and fasting which will help us maintain our spiritual balance. Most importantly, as often as you put physical food into your mouth you should also aim to feed your spiritual body by praying and feasting on the word. Sometimes it is difficult to stay motivated or to stay disciplined with reading your bible, fasting or praying. Warfare is challenging, so keep in mind that preparing yourself will also pose a challenge as well. If you are having trouble staying consistent in the word, try praying with a partner or form a group of three or four. Bear in mind that your prayer partners are not the source so you should not solely or wholeheartedly rely on them, as disappointment is inevitable when it comes to human flesh. As a matter of fact, there will be times when they are unable to pray with you due to scheduling or some other situation. What should you do? Go pray by yourself. He will not give you a cold shoulder when you approach him alone and you will not see a "Will be back soon" or a "Close" sign. No other person place, power or thing on earth can do for us what the Lord can do. God, only, is the author and finisher of our faith.

A Call to Salvation

Dearly beloved, we are living in perilous and dangerous times. I would love to tell you that the times will get better but unfortunately, it will not. However, there is coming a day when a temporary world peace will deceive men into believing all is well, causing them to become complacent and lose focus. Paul reiterates it in 1Thessalonians3:5 that when you think it is peace and safety, it will be sudden destruction. Also be reminded that prior to the return of Jesus Christ, human beings will exhibit the same behavior as they did in the days of Noah. The New International Version of Matthew 24:37 states that "As it was in the days of Noah, so it will be at the coming of the son of man." What does this mean? It means that while God is patiently pleading; warning, and showing us signs and mercy, we still take no heed. Our hearts are hardened leaving us unprepared. We mock God, failing to believe that there will be a second coming followed by the judgment. Presumptuously; we insist on doing things our way craving earthly possessions, seeking fame, building platforms to establish our names, organizing parties and partaking in all sorts of ungodly entertainment. Finally, in the last days we will see atrocities escalading like never before. Our love and commitment has deteriorated. Our genuine affection towards each other is watered down and we are no longer committed to the unity of love through the institution of marriage. Our divorce rates have skyrocketed to an all time high. Everyone wants to walk in his own way or independently act on his own behalf operating with selfishness as the core of his values. As it was in the days of Noah; so it is we rebelliously reject the call of God unto safety and salvation. Therefore, destruction shall be our portion if we do not adhere to the commands of God.

I heard a preacher once say that the people who helped Noah built the ark perished in the flood. What if the statement is true? The same could be said for some believers today who willingly give of themselves, sacrificing their time and energy to build the body of Christ but will not reap the rewards of their labor. What if you are one of those who helped to build the church, established ministry, ensured all departments are well organized and assignments are executed properly but you end up missing God? How sad if on judgment day you hear, "Depart from me I **NEVER** knew you?" Would it not be devastatingly disappointing to know that after investing all your time and energy, giving up all the pleasures of the world to do God's work and lead His people, you are not eligible to inherit the eternal benefits? Rather, you are being rerouted eternal damnation. Do not misunderstand; It's not God's will for any of us to be separated from Him. He has given us a free will to choose. Where we end up will be the result of our choices. In Deuteronomy 30:15, God said "I set before you life and death . . . choose life."

Friends, we have been informed throughout the bible and have seen signs of Christ second coming. Every story and every word written in the bible is for us to emulate the good, reject the bad and learn not to make the same sinful mistakes. It is for us to acquire knowledge and be equipped for our journey. Remember, it is written man shall not live by bread alone but by *every word* spoken by God. Take heed to the story of the five foolish virgins referenced in Matthew 25. If you are not ready, it is time to get ready. Now is the time for you to seek salvation. It is time to get your house in order so you can grow and allow the anointing to flow. Be watchful: step out of your comfort zone and get rid of your complacent attitude. From January to December we know which holidays are coming so we prepare and celebrate. Sadly though, after hearing and seeing all the signs pointing to the return of Christ, we still refuse to prepare ourselves for Him. We do not know the chaos that is on the horizon and the return of Jesus Christ is closer than we can imagine. Brothers and sisters, if you have not been saved and born-again, I urge you to say yes to Jesus today and start running the Christian race with urgency. May I remind you, Christianity is not a religion it is a relationship with Jesus Christ. In John 14: 6, Jesus says, "I am the way, the truth, and the life: no man cometh to the father, but by me." He did not come for the righteous but to call sinners to repentance. Yes, the race will not be free of troubles but you will be able to enjoy the abundance of joy from being in His presence.

Saints or sinners, I admonish you to stop playing and start praying. If it were God's intention for us to perish, He would not have taken the time to robe himself in flesh, come on earth and endure humiliation, sufferings, ostracism and death for you and I. In our sinful state of corruption, He negotiated and ransomed His life for ours. Beloved, you are loved beyond comparison. On the flip side of that equation, there is an adversary at work. Whether or not you believe it, receive it or acknowledge it, the devil and his demons are real and there is a set aside place where he and his followers will spend eternity. Satan is not your friend no matter what you do for him or how much you allow him to use you. He is very successful at what he does because he is organized and persistent.

The choice is yours today. I hear some people say they do not want to participate in Christianity or any religion for that matter. They just want to live a normal life. I say to you, do not allow the devil deceive you. Not making a choice is in fact a conscious choice. Some things are just the way they are and we will have no knowledge of this mystery until the Lord reveals it to us in glory. Just because I do not understand the mystery of fire does not mean it will not continue to burn. So it is with salvation, we may not understand all it entails but if we choose to be on the side of Jesus Christ, we are on the winning side. Why not choose to be victorious. Again, the choice is yours. Make the right one.

Prayer

Oh Lord I give you thanks and praise, honor and glory for your divine intervention in this project. Thank you for the revelation, inspiration and information you have given me to complete my first book. Precious Lord, help me to live what I speak, teach, preach and write. Keep me humble in the sight of men and in your hand. Father, continue to fill me with valuable information so I will be able to share with your people. Mighty God, I ask you for extraordinary blessings and uncommon favor upon all individuals holding this book and for those who have sown into this ministry. Lord, give a listening ear and a receptive heart to this reader while he or she is reading this book so they can hear your voice and follow your direction clearly in Jesus name.

Heavenly Father, decree and I declare that this reader's needs be met right now in the name of Jesus. Lord, I command all sickness to disappear now from this reader's body in Jesus name. God you said in your word that healing is your children's bread and you have sent your word to heal. Jehovah Raphe, you are the healer and if this reader is suffering from cancer; diabetes, asthma, or any other diseases known to man, I bind them up and strip them from their assignment. Father, I come against every lung condition, cancer, kidney disease, every rare blood disease, muscle or joint pain, abdominal or intestinal conditions in Jesus mighty name. Glaucoma, deafness, high blood pressure, or any abnormality in the body I command you through the power of God to leave this body now. I render you powerless and I cast you out to outer darkness in Jesus name. Father I replace every spirit of affliction and infirmity with the spirit of healing, joy, peace and deliverance.

Mighty God of Zion, through the power in the blood of Jesus, I speak to every financial drought in your life. There shall be no more lack in Jesus name. I call forth financial blessings from the East, West, North, and South and any money that's been owed to you, I command the borrower to return it now in Jesus name.

Holy Spirit, every marriage that you ordained I command them to line up with your promise that no man shall put them asunder. I come against third-party interferences seeking to destroy your marriage today. I come against the spirit of neglect. I rebuke the fowl spirits that tries to tear this marriage apart in Jesus name. Every argumentative spirit I command you to hold your peace in Jesus name. I speak love, respect, honor and friendship in this marriage right now through Jesus Christ our Lord.

Lord, I pray for the family of this reader and if there are children Lord, I ask that you intervene with salvation, protection, and deliverance from the traps of the enemy. Every plot, fiery dart, and arrow I send them back to the into the enemy's camp in Jesus name. Lord let their family escape unharmed and let them know that you are the one who keeps and protects them. Father, if there is a need that I fail to mention, fail not to grant it in Jesus name. Lord, regulate the mind of those who are confused and draw closer to those who are sold out for you in Jesus name amen.

A Note of Thanks

With heart-felt gratitude, I would like to say thank you for purchasing this book. Thank you for inviting me in your homes, cars, churches, place of work and hotel room or wherever you may be when reading this book. Thank you for listening.

It is a pleasure to share with you God's amazing answers to prayers. It is to reassure you that God can use you mightily if you draw closer to Him through the power of prayer.

There is much more to God's miracles than what you have read but in order for you to experience Him in His fullness and partake of His Glory, you must put the principles of the book in action by applying it to your life on a daily basis. To get results you must pray, praise, worship and fast. You have to step away and detach yourself from rituals, religion, and tradition then aim your thoughts on the positive.

I challenge you today that if you make prayer a priority in your life and esteem it above everything else, you will experience the power of God in your life like never before. Fear not folks, there is still power in prayer!

References

Baker, Warren, and Eugene E. Carpenter. *The Complete Word Study Dictionary: Old Testament.* AMG Publishers. 2003. Print.

Holt, Steven. "The Power of Fasting and Prayer." Web. 19 Dec. 2012. *http://steveaholt.wordpress.com.*

"The Tabernacle." Used with permission from Goodseed International, 2000. Web. 23 March 2013. www.goodseed.com.

About the Author

*J*asmine Gordon is no ordinary individual. Dubbed the "firewoman" by friends and family, she is known in the gospel arena to be a woman on fire for the Lord. It is this passionate fire igniting from within that lead Jasmine down a pathway destined to reveal her true fate.

Jasmine, born as Nichole Gordon on the Island of Jamaica is the seventh of nine children. Having been raised in a Christian home she grew up with the fear of God so it was only fitting that she would embark on a spiritual journey that would eventually lead her to add author to her growing list of credentials. Jasmine earned her education in Evangelism at the Manhattan Bible Institute in New York and travels as an international Evangelist. Not only is Jasmine an aspiring author, she is also a radio personality as well as a gospel recording artist, earning the coveted title of "Best Original Song" in 2005 on the Gil Bailey Gospel Awards show for her song entitled "I'm on Fire." She went on to record three other gospel albums as well as two CD recordings on prayer.

Jasmine talents span across many fields. She is the founder and Ambassador for Ministries without Boundaries, a non-profit organization where she ministers to the material needs of others. Since May 2011, on Mother and Father's day she was able to put a smile on the faces of mothers and fathers in her community by hosting an annual concert and banquet in honor of parents, free of charge. She strongly believes if earthly needs are met, it will incline the listener to hear her message. With such busy schedule, Jasmine still finds time to do what she refers to as her secular ministry, which is professional nursing.

Ten years ago, Jasmine was inspired by the Holy Spirit to pen her experiences through the power of prayer, which resulted in her book entitled "Fear Not, There Is Still Power in Prayer." This book is written to transform doubters into believers, to reinforce the value and importance of prayer, to encourage believers to keep on praying and to teach others how to pray. As an intercessor, she knows that there is still power in prayer, which is second nature to her. Jasmine prayers instantaneously affect the powers of darkness and set captives free. The most joyous time in her life is receiving prayer request from individuals all over the world and hearing their testimonies of deliverance. She will never stop praying until something happens.

Jasmine will confess that she does not know all the answers nor does she know where and how ends will meet sometimes. But she has an everlasting faith that has moved mountainous situation out of her life. She may not be a highly acclaimed celebrity but to those who know her and have been touched by her presence and ministries know that indeed she may be the next legendary philanthropist in her community. She is always trying to make someone smile. A woman on fire for the Lord and devoted to His guidance, what will she do next!

Jasmine presently resides in Palm Bay Florida and is the proud mother of one child, Javin.